LONESOME RHODES

One man
two wheels
and 19,000 miles

Ashley Rhodes

Published by Sigma Leisure – an imprint of
Sigma Press, 1 South Oak Lane, Wilmslow, Cheshire SK9 6AR, England.

British Library Cataloguing in Publication Data
A CIP record for this book is available from the British Library.

ISBN: 1 85058 782 5

Typesetting and Design by: Sigma Press, Wilmslow, Cheshire.

Cover Design: The Agency, Macclesfield

Cover photographs: the author

Photographs: the author

Route map: Bute Cartographics

Printed by: MFP Design & Print

Foreword
– by William Roache MBE

For forty-two years, I have been part of 'Coronation Street' – so much so that some people think that I really am Ken Barlow! But as Shakespeare said "All the world's a stage, and all the men and women merely players" so perhaps what really matters is what we do in the world when we're not working at our day jobs – when we can be our true selves and achieve our ambitions beyond the 9 to 5.

In this respect, I have been fortunate in that not only has my acting career been enormously rewarding, but also I have been able to get involved in supporting many good causes. I have been particularly pleased to support the David Lewis Centre – a world-famous establishment for the care and treatment of epilepsy sufferers, set in the Cheshire countryside.

I live in Wilmslow, a pleasant suburban town a few miles south of Manchester, and Ashley owned a hairdressing salon nearby. It is more years than I care to remember since I first had my hair cut by Ashley, but I do clearly remember the many interesting and unusual conversations. He was not at all like the unfair stereotype of his profession, with a collection of girlfriends, a love of fast cars and motorbikes – and a passion for travel. We soon began to read in the local newspaper about his exploits – about how he was importing American cars and riding his motorbike to far-flung places.

I was fascinated by Ashley's adventures and at first a little envious! But I did not envy him at all when he announced that he intended to ride a motorbike the entire 19,000 miles of the Americas. This was to be his next big adventure and a chance for him to emulate his hero Ted Simon. I was pleased for Ashley, and even more pleased that the David Lewis Centre was to benefit from sponsorship and fund-raising for this epic ride.

Travel can be interesting, exciting and fun. But though it might seem a great idea to ride across the Americas, I'm willing to bet that few of us would be up to the challenges and dangers that faced Ashley: near misses on roads barely worthy of the name, meetings with dubious individuals intent on stealing your possessions, encounters with corrupt officials and stays in seedy hotels with cockroaches for company. I began to feel that I did not envy Ashley for one moment.

Not only did Ashley complete his journey – he lived to tell the tale. On his return, he continued tirelessly to raise money for the David Lewis Centre. He gave talks and slide shows, organised the venues, cajoled people to attend and sold them the tickets. He worked almost single-handedly for a worthwhile cause. And for those unable to attend his talks, he even found time to write this excellent book in which his remarkable experiences are described so entertainingly

Over the years, Ashley Rhodes has transformed himself from a Wilmslow hairdresser to a world-class travel writer. Read on and enjoy his wonderful story. For me, this is a classic of travel writing – and yet a further means of raising money for Ashley's favourite charity.

William Roache

Prologue

Ted Simon completed his legendary four-year trek around the world on a motorcycle when I was a gauche sixteen-year-old and the proud owner of a Suzuki AP50 'sixteener special' sports moped ... complete with pedals! Four short years later, I'd been around the world myself, albeit in the sanitised cocoon of a luxury cruise liner, on which I plied my trade as a hairdresser.

As a 21-year-old veteran of a long list of countries, none of which I'd spent longer in than two days, I picked up a copy of 'Jupiter's Travels' and devoured every word of it, imagining it was the wheels of my bike pounding through deserts, over mountain passes; boldly going where no man had gone before ...

Almost twenty years later, having just reached forty, roughly the age that Ted had been when he'd decided to abandon his fate to the will of God, here I was, ready to do the same. Well, not quite the same, but 19,000 miles is 19,000 miles. It still equates to roughly half the circumference of the world, and anybody who tells you it's easy is lying.

The world has changed a lot in twenty years; politics change, poor countries get poorer, rich ones get richer (in most cases), crime grows as the chasm between the haves and have-nots widens. But, thankfully, motorcycles just get better and better, meaning that I shouldn't have to strip my steed down and rebuild it each time I stopped for petrol. Credit cards, improved telecommunications and banking systems meant I shouldn't be waiting for a month in some malaria-ridden hell-hole for my stolen belongings to be reimbursed. The luxury of purpose-made, all-weather motorcycle clothing saved me from resorting to a sweaty leather 'Ted-style' flying jacket as I blazed my way through the tropics.

I'd completed a 6,500 mile trip to the Middle East four years previously, along with countless European rides, so I had a good idea about the potential risks of such a venture and what it felt like to sit on a motorcycle for days on end; what loneliness would feel like on the lonesome roads of the world's longest continual land mass ... the Americas.

Ashley Rhodes

Acknowledgements

Mike & Gay Rhodes
Staff & Clients of Ashley Rhodes Hairdressing
Friends & Sponsors
William Roache
Sue Murphy, Linda Ashe & Directors, Staff & Residents of the
    David Lewis Centre
Louise Ross & Carrier Travel (Cheshire)
Staff of the Royal Bank of Scotland, Wilmslow
Oliver Robinson of Robinson's Brewery
Jane & Staff of Active Images, Wilmslow
Staff of the Royal Geographical Society
The Embassy of Chile, London
Paul Harris of Brox Signs
Cheadle Medical Centre
University of Manchester Occupational Health Department
Michael Lyon & Staff of Allan Jefferies BMW, Shipley,
    Yorkshire
Bradley Park of American Airlines
Jackie Duffy
Paul McKoen
Mike Laughton
David Johnstone
Nigel Barrett
Bracken Motorcycles (Touratech Agents)
Maria Elena Himenez, British Embassy, La Paz
Max Soto of Euro Autos de Centroamerica
Steve Beaudry of Beaudry Motorsports
Cecilia Campos
Elizabeth Arratia Sainz
Marisol Jaramillo
Irene Sanchez
Captain Felix Newbold
Manfred of Cartagena
Mayelys Baldovino, family & staff at Club Nautico, Cartagena
Herman Jonker
Debbie Ann Stultz
Jim Mateer
Zoe Miles
Phil Marvin
Kristen Kemerling
Terry Hirst of Expedition Freight
Doug Wootton of Mannix Freight, Richmond, Vancouver B.C.

Contents

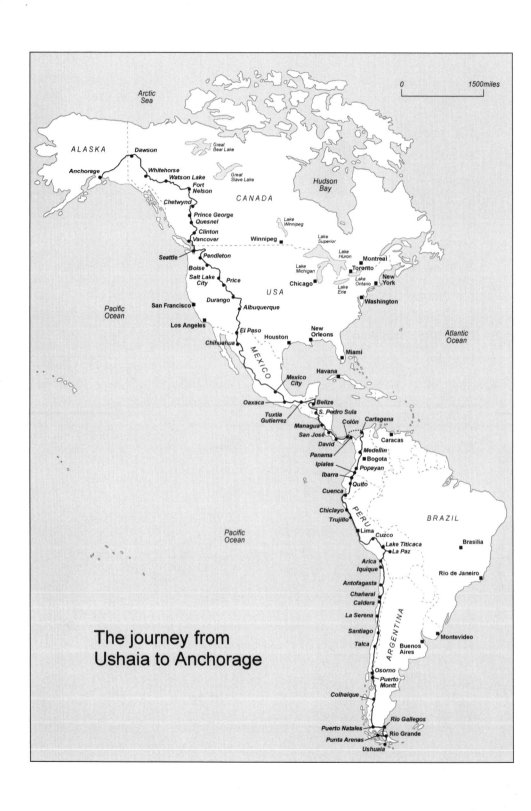

The journey from
Ushaia to Anchorage

Chapter 1

How to Plan an Adventure

Punta Arenas. I roll the name around my mouth savouring its familiarity. I had lost track of the times I had responded to the polite enquiries of friends and well-wishers; "Yes, I start my journey in Punta Arenas, it's the most southerly city in the world actually", quoting the solitary fact I possessed about this lonely, frigid, wind-battered outpost.

It had been a voyage of discovery, the eighteen months of build-up to the present moment, saying awkward farewells to my Mum and Dad and my friend Louise at the check-in at Manchester Airport. Mum looked tearful and emotionally drained. She had convinced herself that I would become a Foreign Office kidnap statistic: "sections of human torso discovered floating down an Amazonian tributary have been identified as belonging to 40-year-old English motorcycle adventurer, Ashley Rhodes". Dad adopted a more sanguine approach, commenting cheerfully that at best, I could expect my bike and all my belongings to be stolen. Louise just sobbed uncontrollably. It did not exactly fill me with hope and optimism.

I owned a hairdressing salon. Not the kind of occupation normally associated with derring-doers in Third World combat zones. Wilmslow, my home, posed no risks, other than temporary blindness as the sun reflects off a thousand Gucci handbag snaffles.

An ex-girlfriend once passed me a back-handed compliment. She said: "Ashley, you're a classy guy with a common streak". My alter ego always seems to point me towards an earthier life.

I'm frequently asked what makes an (almost) middle aged man with a comfortable life and successful business jeopardise it to ride 19,000 miles from Chile to Alaska through a host of dubious looking countries. It started for me about 20 years ago when I read the hugely motivational 'Jupiter's Travels' by Ted Simon. Ted was one of the early pioneers of round-the-world motorcycling. His was a no-frills approach – no satellite phones or GPS units then. I didn't want to replicate his trip to the point where I had to do it on some smoky old oil spewing anachronism from the 'glory days' of British motorcycling – I'm not that masochistic. Neither did I want to be dashing off e-mails from deepest Patagonia on my state-of-the-art hand-held computer thingy. I wanted to feel the earth between my toes, to marvel at its enormity, to subject myself to fear, elation, frustration and joy. But most of all I wanted to taste freedom!

I had tasted freedom four years previously. I had ridden a Triumph Daytona 900 to the Middle East to attend a friend's wedding. I could only spare five weeks for the 6500-mile 15-country trip, but I remember wishing that it would never end. The rougher the countries got – Bulgaria, Romania, Albania – the more elated I felt.

I had made a few mistakes on that trip – not least of which was taking a smoothly shod sports bike to ride some of the world's roughest roads (Albania's). My luggage distribution left a little to be desired, too – a towering periscope of reinforced nylon wobbled uncertainly in front of my chest. I peered over it, straining to see my fuel gauge and speedo. This edifice was my tank bag – the mainstay of my worldly belongings.

My preparations for this trip were much more thorough. The choice of bike was a one-horse race. Everything I had read or was told alluded to the BMW GS being the bike for the job. My earlier rides on this model left me feeling unsure. The immense seat height and wide-set handlebars made me feel like Hannibal of the Alps, though its size soon diminished as I got used to it.

I did a deal for the bike – an unregistered BMW R1100 GS. It came in a rather fetching silver and yellow livery. I had my helmet custom painted to match it, with a big map of the Americas airbrushed onto it, running from side to side. "Now you really look as though you're worth robbing," commented my Mum with weary resignation.

The bike came factory-fitted with anti-lock brakes and heated handlebar grips. I ordered a host of further embellishments from Touratech, a German company who modify BMW GSs for serious overlanding: handguards, crash bars, gearbox and headstock reinforcement, a scroll route planner, headlamp guard and, most importantly, two 35 litre aluminium 'Zega' cases. The obvious advantage of aluminium panniers over other hard luggage is they can generally be re-welded in the event of accident in the most primitive of Third World workshops. The panniers were adorned with a multitude of corporate sponsor stickers.

I sold space on my panniers to a number of companies in exchange for sizeable donations to my selected charity, the David Lewis Centre. The Centre, based in Warford, Cheshire, is a long-established residential school and centre dedicated to epilepsy sufferers, many of whom have associated problems. It caters for both children and adults, with impressive results. It's regarded as one of the leading centres of its kind in the UK.

I had rather rashly announced to Sue Murphy, the head of fund-raising at the Centre, that I was going to raise £20,000 in sponsor-ship for them. I did not fully appreciate the impact this gesture of largesse was to have on my life until I painstakingly sent out 250 carefully worded appeals to the corporate world. I received in return, just one cheque – for 50 quid.

Undeterred, I set about tapping up friends, family and my clients. Owning a hairdressing salon gave me a good pool of poten-tial sponsors. They were generous to a fault. The appeal started to gather momentum, especially when my good Samaritan neigh-bour, Bill Roache, *aka* Coronation Street's Ken Barlow, came on board to give me a good media profile.

Newspapers, magazines and radio stations picked up on the story. I became a legend in my own lunchtime with bylines like: "Daredevil biker, Ashley Rhodes" and "Wilmslow's most famous biker", which is no big deal when you realise there are only half-a-dozen other bikers in the town!

The pressure was building up. I was trying to juggle the running of the business with sending out endless charity appeals. Shipping had to be arranged, documents procured, particularly letters of safe passage, an invaluable aid in tricky situations, but notoriously hard to obtain. Vaccinations, banking arrangements, extra Spanish lessons, learning simple bike maintenance, amassing vital equip-ment, route planning, risk assessment: the list was endless.

I made dozens of trips to London. Being a Fellow of the Royal Geographical Society, I spent hours in their map room and library, soaking up any morsel of useful information.

I trudged around the embassies in the late autumn. It's dispirit-ing to be given the runaround by some jumped-up petty bureaucrat hiding behind his nation's flag: "We can't see you now. Come back in two hours." "Our visa department is open between 11.00 and 11.30 then they close for lunch for four hours." "Go away you irritating Englishman." The last quoted is not quite true, but it may as well have been.

The insides of the embassies seemed to reflect the perception of the country's character. Peru was tatty, hand-me-down furniture and the odd poncho. Colombia's was menacing-looking men in tight shiny suits with an implied whiff of drug money.

*   *   *   *

My bike was to be despatched to the docks at Felixstowe eight weeks prior to my arrival in Chile. Expedition freight in Hull had located a cargo ship bound for Valparaiso in Chile. The bike would then be transferred to another ship which would take it on to Punta Arenas.

Terry Hirst, MD of Expedition Freight, forwarded the various bills of lading, insurance documents etc. which I passed onto Michael Lyon, Service Director of Allan Jefferies, a BMW dealership in Shipley, Yorkshire. I had bought my bike from them because, as a young teenager visiting my grandmother who lived nearby, I spent much of my time gazing wistfully through their showroom windows. They loaded the bike into a purpose-built BMW crate and trucked it down to Felixstowe. I prayed for two months that my beloved bike would turn up at the other end, on time and intact. I knew that if it missed its Valparaiso connection it would take anything up to a month to find a suitable on-going vessel. My trip would be sabotaged before it had even begun.

I had only managed one brief dry run on the bike, fully laden. Now it was gone, all I could do was finely hone my packaging skills. I could not afford any extraneous matter in those pannier liners. My clothing for four months would have to be restricted to one pair of shoes, one pair of trainers, one pair of sandals, along with two pairs of trousers, two pairs of shorts, six T-shirts, an assortment of underwear and thermals, and one fine-knit pullover. A comprehensive medical kit included an assortment of gruesome looking syringes. "I don't know why you're taking these. You can't stand the sight of needles," Louise said reassuringly. "Yes, but don't you see? They make me feel like a man on a mission!" I replied. In truth,

Clean, shiny and ready for the off: outside the David Lewis Centre with
Coronation Street's William Roache and Louise Ross of Carrier Travel

if the likelihood of injections arose, I would be straight on the
phone to my insurance company for an immediate airlift.

The only items I really knew how to use were my assorted
courses of pills. Beyond the inevitable anti-malaria tablets I carried
a host of anti-bacterial tablets and multi-vitamins. The former
supposedly to kill any bugs in the digestive tract before they had
the chance to take hold.

I was more concerned with dangers to my health caused by
gun-toting guerillas than any perceived risks to my large intestine. I
took out some heavy anti-kidnap insurance in addition to an
all-risks 'dangerous activities' policy. Insurance for the bike could
not be arranged from England, other than while at sea. I was told I
could insure the bike on a third party only basis for each country,
payable at the border. I greatly doubted the validity of such a policy
so decided to adopt the normal developing world scheme of things.
You run over a cow and it's $100 to the owner, ranging down to a
chicken at about five bucks, arbitrated by the local policeman.

The last fortnight prior to departure was a whirlwind of frantic
phone calls, farewells, writing lists, planning and more planning –
and a nagging sense of unease about my personal safety. I had
received a fax via a client of mine from the president of Colombia's
main bank with whom she is friendly. It read: "Tell your friend on

NO account must he ride his motorcycle through Colombia. This would be most unsafe". I decided to ignore the advice and plough on with my plans to take a boat from the north coast of Colombia to Panama, having ridden through the country in its entirety.

I foolishly left the fax lying around on my desk where my mother spotted it. "Oh, God! You're not going through there are you?" she exclaimed in horror. I made a few placatory noises and told her I'd "be careful". I think by then her vision of my butchered torso floating down the Amazon had been superseded by one of combat-fatigued guerillas holding AK47s to my head.

We'd said all we needed to say, hugged and kissed. I was on my way. Eighteen months of planning culminates here – at the check-in-desk.

Sipping a coffee in the airport, I thought about the mission ahead of me. It would take me two days to get to Punta Arenas by air. Unfortunately, the Miami flight arrived at Santiago de Chile half-an-hour after the daily flight departed for Punta Arenas, creating a further delay. I would collect my bike at Punta Arenas and take the ferry on to Tierra del Fuego and the 300 or so miles down to Ushuaia, Argentina: the most southerly town in the world and my official starting point. From there, the only way is up: Argentina, Chile, Bolivia, Peru, Ecuador, Colombia, Panama, Costa Rica, Nicaragua, Honduras, Belize, Guatemala, Mexico, the United States of Texas, New Mexico, Colorado, Utah, Idaho, Oregon, Washington, the Canadian Provinces of British Colombia and Yukon Territory, and finally ... Alaska. It made me weary just *reading* the list. My estimate for this distance was about 19,000 miles.

On the British Airways shuttle to Heathrow the stewardess enquired as to whether I was going on holiday. I explained that I was embarking on a mammoth charity ride. I must have done a good job of singing my virtues because she offered to get me a free upgrade on the London-Miami leg. Regrettably I had to tell her that my pal, Bradley, who marketed the airline, had already taken care of it.

The stewardess was a Liverpudlian. Did you know that the people of Liverpool and Belfast make more independent charitable donations than any other part of the UK?

*   *   *   *

Flicking through *El Nuevo Herald* while whiling away seven

deadly hours in one of Miami Airport's dreariest restaurants, I read that the Fuerzas Armadas Revolucionarias de Colombia (FARC) were on another murdering spree. Images of Colombia were beginning to haunt me.

Exhausted and bored witless I sit through another three-hour delay. Watching the Chileans board the American Airlines flight to Santiago, I'm curious to note how stylish they look. An oasis of elegance in a desert of tennis shoes and wrinkle-free chinos. They're so much paler than other Latin Americans. The women scrape their glossy black tresses away from their faces. Their complexions are almost creamy, their features Southern European. I had heard that Chile's economy was similar to that of Wales – but they sure didn't look like that in Colwyn Bay.

Chapter 2

Destination Loneliness

The descent into Santiago, over the Andes is one of life's wonders. I marvelled at this spine of snow-capped peaks, running the length of South America. The airport stretched into infinity, eventually merging into some fearsome looking mountains. Bussing into the centre was a somewhat less awe-inspiring event – miles of temporary looking discount shops and tyre depots.

I collapsed, exhausted, on to the faded counterpane in the pleasantly down-at-heel Hotel Conde Ansurez, located in the heart of the old centre. I had always convinced myself that a few concessions in the luxury stakes were worthwhile when compared to being isolated in a better hotel on the edge of town.

Avenida O'Higgins bisects the city of Santiago. A broad two-lane boulevard with a verdant median. Named after Chile's illustrious liberator, the unlikely named General Bernardo O'Higgins, it forms a reference point for the whole of the city. On this autumnal Sunday afternoon I strolled a good part of its length. Young couples were out in force: holding hands, kissing and generally looking enraptured. Santiago is an expensive city so most courtships take place in public parks – because they're free.

The architecture is an odd mix of almost modern, sixties brutalist granite and the odd lovely colonial building. There's a 'settled' atmosphere in Santiago, something uncharacteristic of Latin America. Chile is frequently hailed as South America's success story though not without its growing pains. Between 1973 and 1981 policies were introduced to bring inflation down from in excess of 500 per cent to under 10 per cent. Although fiscal balance was achieved the Chileans were left with an overvalued peso. In the early 1980s they battled against further inflation caused by the freeing of the exchange rate. Attempts to curb it resulted in a deep recession. Chile fought its way out of this black hole by restructuring its debt packages and more recently by increased G.D.P and improved exports.

Trudging for seemingly miles down Avenida O'Higgins, I found an interesting little park, actually more like a citadel of rock, called Cerro Santa Lucia. This is about 70 metres high with observation points at the top. I'm sure the views from the telescopes would have been great were it not for the habitual smog that lingers over Santiago. The city has one of the poorest air qualities on earth.

I wandered aimlessly down Avenida O'Higgins for hours trying to find the epicentre of the action to no avail. I was told it all happened out in the rich suburbs of Las Condes and Providencia. I gave up and ate a *pichanga*, a type of mixed grill in a modest little *comedor* (diner). No problems with beef-on-the-bone out here.

After a fitful sleep dominated by dreams (or nightmares, depending on your politics) of General Pinochet and tanks rumbling down Avenida O'Higgins, I rose at 5.00 a.m. for the 7.45 flight to Punta Arenas via Puerto Montt. "Su billete es por Avant" the girl on the Lanchile check-in informed me, directing me to Chile's third largest airline, and consequently its smallest. Fortunately my plane had been bought second-hand from Britannia, not Aeroflot as once happened to me in Honduras.

Mulling over the possible scenarios that would greet me in Punta Arenas made me increasingly apprehensive of finding my bike alive and well. In the early 1990s I had imported a few old Chevrolet Corvettes from the USA into Liverpool. The paperwork had been endless. Now Scouse is a fairly unfamiliar lingo if you're from Cheshire, but not as obscure as Chilean Spanish, which is spoken with the speed of a Gatling gun.

I tried to divert my mind onto the landscape below. It was flat, green and waterlogged – featureless, other than for the odd *estancia* (ranch). As the aircraft door was opened for embarking passengers at Puerto Montt, a gust of frigid air whipped into the cabin. It could not be much over freezing point. Images of uncrating my bike on a lonesome quayside, armed only with a Swiss army knife in a force ten gale preoccupied me.

Punta Arenas is in the bottom third of a country that stretches for 4,329 kilometres from top to bottom and averages 180 kilometres in width. The fact that only one per cent of Chile's human population live in this bottom third, yet co-exist with 50 per cent of the country's sheep told me where my prevailing love-interest might lie.

The 'fifth zone', as the area stretching from Puerto Montt to Cape Horn is known, is a region of fjords, forests, mountains and glaciers. What little population there is, consists mainly of Mestizos (mixed Spanish and Indian blood), Croats, British and, further up in the Lake District, a small colony of Germans. British expatriates usually leave our country for sunnier climes. Not in this case. The western edge of Patagonia is one of the wettest areas on the planet.

It suddenly struck me. I had been on the plane for almost four hours and still hadn't reached Punta Arenas. I knew practically all the roads in the fifth zone were *ripio* (gravel roads). I would have a struggle to cover the 1,500 miles or so back to Santiago allied with the 500 mile round trip across Tierra del Fuego plus return ferries in much less than a fortnight. I was going to have to scrap the five-day Spanish course I had planned for Santiago – not enough time.

*   *   *   *

Arriving in Punta Arenas was a real culture shock. I wrestled my huge suitcase off the single carousel in this one-horse airport and into the boot of an ancient Daewoo taxi. We bounced along rutted gravel tracks through a lunar landscape. The sky was washed a bleak pale grey. Lionel, my equally ancient taxi driver had a leathery creased face that suggested too many Patagonian winters. He took me directly to the *Oficines Maritimas*. It was closed. The May Day holiday meant that the whole city felt even more like a ghost town than usual.

Heading back into town, we passed continual jerry-built corrugated iron houses painted in a rich palette of colours. Despite being a city of 100,000 inhabitants, none of them looked as though they were staying long. The appearance is one of impermanence – like a township.

Despite my disappointment about having to wait till the following day, the bitter wind and lifeless streets I was itching to explore this bizarre city.

Lionel dropped me off at a predictably crappy hotel; $37 with a cot-like bed, non-functioning toilet and a broken heating system. As the season was so short, the hoteliers in Punta Arenas were clearly capitalising on their brief window of opportunity. Thirty-seven bucks is extortion.

The town isn't the last word in excitement. The best entertainment on offer was a prize-giving ceremony to a bunch of junior marathon winners, held in the local park: a dainty, genteel oasis of wrought iron, marigolds and lupins.

I stumbled into a warm, welcoming restaurant for lunch – not that the outside gave that impression, looking like a derelict fish-canning plant. The grilled *congrio* or conger eel was delicious. In this format served simply with chips and salad, though conger eel can be eaten numerous ways in Chile, it is the closest they have to a national dish: in soup, stew or simply grilled. I started with 'consomme con huevo', where the egg is cooked by the heat of soup, in the style of Spain's 'Sopa Castellano'. Seafood is excellent in Chile, though I always avoided the mussels, which eaten at the wrong time of year can carry the 'marea roja' (red tide) disease which can be fatal to humans.

The waiter, with great ceremony, offered me a book of their elegant matches in exchange for my crumpled Pizza Express ones.

Punta Arenas is how I imagine Port Stanley in the Falklands would look with its fifties style weather-beaten clapboard houses. I had mentioned this to Lionel, but I had referred to them by their Argentinian name of Las Malvinas, thinking he would understand me better. "No son Las Malvinas – son Las Islas FALKLAND!" he

Tierra del Fuego: some Argentinians are still fighting the Falklands War

retorted sharply. I had felt a strong empathy from Chilean people towards the English though it had probably been eroded somewhat by Jack Straw's bungled attempts to bring their ex-president to justice. Despite Pinochet's low popularity in Chile, I don't think Chileans welcomed our interference in their affairs.

*   *   *   *

I presented myself at the docks the following morning armed with reams of paperwork connecting me to my bike. After being escorted to the main office by a noncommittal freight forwarder, I embarked on a five-hour paper trail being dragged from office to office for endless meaningless rubber stamps, by an impish looking young gopher called Fernando. We ran into an obstacle which meant a ride out of town in a *colectivo* (shared taxi) followed by a three-kilometre walk.

Pitching up at this remote customs shed my patience was wearing thin, not helped by the bloated hatchet-faced official who looked upon Fernando with disdain and me with complete indifference. I could tell by Fernando's deference that the likelihood of leaving Punta Arenas with my bike any time within the next month rested with this odious man.

We stood patiently while hatchet-face reclined in his chair, yawned, belched, scratched his crotch and minutely inspected his finger nails. After 30 minutes of this treatment he sighed and picked up my passport. He found the fact that my name was the same as that of his watch amusing. He wrote my clearance papers out in the name of Ashley 'Citizen' Rhodes.

Returning to the port I was eventually reunited with my absent friend. There was my bike alone in its crate in a huge shed. A helpful dock worker, Fernando and I set about uncrating and rebuilding the bike. Standing there in all its previous glory, there was just one problem: I couldn't find the keys! I made a couple of long-distance calls to Mick Lyon at Allan Jefferies. No, he could not remember where they were hidden either. We eventually discovered them secreted under the sump bash plate.

I signed off a couple more meaningless chits, thanked my helpers profusely and rode triumphantly out of the dock gates in the direction of Tres Puentes on the outskirts of town. It was from here that I would take the ferry to Tierra del Fuego the following day.

Back at the hotel I gave a delighted chambermaid my Delsey

suitcase and grip, decanted all my belongings into my panniers and checked out in favour of a more comfortable gaff round the corner, picking up an extortionately priced road map of southern Patagonia on the way. It proved worth its weight in gold, having every all-important fuel stop marked.

The desk clerk at the Hotel Finis Terrae gave me a $19 discount without prompting in deference to the monumental task that faced me. Having not eaten for 24 hours due to my total absorption with clearing the bike, I gorged myself on a dozen *empanadas con pino* (meat turnovers) and *empanadas con queso* (with cheese) washed down with a couple of Cerveza Astrals 'from the world's most southerly brewery'.

I turned up for the ferry at daybreak. My fellow passengers were gathered around the little wooden ticket hut, which doubled as a snack bar. The only building on the quayside. A short, squat, hardy looking bunch, they were considerably less animated than one expects from South American people. A mixture of mutual respect and reserve prevents them from making a fuss of strangers, however alien they look, and I looked *very* alien. They merely observed me with mild curiosity from under the brims of their pork-pie hats. There's certainly a lack of hustlers and in-your-face merchants to be found in the more northerly Andean countries.

It was an eerie sight that greeted me as the rusty old ferry berthed at Porvenir, Tierra del Fuego. If Punta Arenas is like the moon, then this is Mars. Wild and rugged with a permanently malevolent sky, it gave me a thrill of anticipation.

The first 150 kilometres or so is Chilean territory, after that the eastern half of the island is governed by Argentina as testified by large placards declaring: "Malvinas por Argentina"!

Humans are scarce, adding to the haunting beauty of the 'Land of Fire'. Only gulls exist in any number, soaring and swooping over the dark icy sea.

I had never really done much off-road riding, so was apprehensive about the all-ripio roads and trails. I approached them gingerly at about 20 mph, clenching my buttocks and hanging on for grim death. The bike slewed around wildly, convincing me that this was not the style to adopt. I tried again, gradually upping my gear and speed, gently counter-steering round bends, gripping the bars very lightly. At 60 mph in fourth gear I found the perfect balance of speed and traction, allowing the back wheel to weave gently. I was

The official starting point: Ushuaia, Tierra del Fuego

right in the swing of it – riding, like a would-be wall-of-death rider, the hard shoulder that banked the side of the road.

Rio Grande is the principal town of the island. An ugly sprawling affair with Iron Curtain sculptures. I found the town depressing, not helped by the endless rain and dour inhabitants. Despite the onset of dusk, I flipped a mental coin and opted for the long ride on to Ushuaia.

The temperature plummeted as I climbed up to the Garibaldi Pass. Trucks kicked out dense clouds of dust that clung to my damp visor, rendering me temporarily blind in the pitch black of the mountains. Big flakes of snow started to fall. I thanked God that it was a gravel road, which offered me a modicum of grip under the layer of snow.

I limped into Ushuaia at 10.00 p.m. – fourteen hours after catching the ferry from Tres Puentes. Despite my freezing extremities my heart was soaring. I was here! Ushuaia. The last town in the world. I felt as though I had completed something, even though my ride had not officially begun.

Chapter 3

The End of the World

I stopped to ask a woman directions to the Hotel Cabo de Hornos. She tried to talk me into staying at her father's *casa de huespedes* (guest house). I took a look at it, decided that all my prospective fellow residents had a propensity to either murder or suicide and couldn't envisage sharing a bathroom with any of them, so wound up at the Cabo de Hornos anyway. I turned up at the hotel in a filthy state but was accepted with good grace.

Taking a midnight stroll down the main street, I was struck by the high quality duty-free goods in the shops and the amount of choice. There were things that you might actually want to buy, especially after the meagre offerings of Punta Arenas. The buildings were of similar clapboard type but attractively sloped down to the seafront, San Francisco style. I decided that this was a place that well-heeled Argentineans might come to in summer.

I had the arduous task of sluicing down all my equipment before exploring Ushuaia. My plastic waterproofs were so filthy I had to wear them in the shower. A casual observer seeing me naked but for a black plastic oversuit may have thought they were witnessing a 'special interest' porn video.

It takes a long time for light to arrive on Tierra del Fuego in autumn but it was worth the wait. Having arrived in the pitch black, I had no idea of the beauty of Ushuaia's setting. The town nestles at the foot of jutting snow-capped peaks on three sides, the fourth being the Beagle Channel, looking across to Antarctica. A small port forms the focal point of the bay. In it sat a pair of Argentine naval frigates, their battleship grey livery merging with the anthracite depths of the Beagle Channel.

I literally raced down to the beach with my cameras to capture the mist-shrouded peaks. Little did I realise they stay shrouded all day. After amusing myself for an hour with tripods and suchlike, I collected the bike to ride the final 22 kilometres to the end of Ruta 3 – the road to the end of the world. This was the end of the road and here were the placards to prove it, set in the midst of a stunningly beautiful national park.

Setting my camera to auto-timer I photographed myself in various sponsors' T-shirts. Small groups of Argentine tourists along with the odd North American exclaimed with incredulity when I told them what I was attempting. I had no self-doubts. I was brimming with confidence.

Back in town I visited the Museo Fin del Mundo (Museum at the End of the World), not least because they will stamp your passport accordingly. Being a little vain, I like a well-stamped passport. The museum focuses on native Fuegian tribes, in particular the Yamana. It was their fires that the Portuguese explorer, Ferdinand Magellan, first observed in 1520 when he discovered the Island. The fires were the means used by the native Indians used to warn each other of an alien sighting. Magellan consequently referred to "Tierra del Humo" or Land of Smoke, which was later modified by Charles V of Spain to Tierra del Fuego. Sadly, there are no pure-blooded Indians on the island now. They had no immunity to the diseases introduced by white settlers and were mainly killed off by measles and tuberculosis.

As morning light washed over Ushuaia I lay in bed contemplating the nine-hour ride ahead of me to catch the last ferry off the island. With rain beating against my window and a pervasive chill in the air, I knew a grim day was in store.

The dirt road climbed up to the Garibaldi Pass. Miles of roadworks turned it into a quagmire, negotiable only in second gear and by feathering the clutch. Only two hours out of Ushuaia I stopped for a rest, mentally drained by the intense concentration and covered head to toe in thick slurry. A pack of wild dogs ran towards me. They circled me growling savagely. I was too weary to react. They soon got bored and wandered off, supporting the theory that you should never show a dog you're frightened of it.

The road to Rio Grande was blocked by two large fires and a gang of men picketing. Trying to outwit them I rode across some wasteland. I managed to bury myself in a gravel trap necessitating much pushing and shoving of my 250 kilo bike – much to the amusement of the work-to-rule boys.

After a gas station microwave lunch and a welcome opportunity

Nowheresville – on Ruta 3

to thaw out my freezing feet, I tackled the leg north of Rio Grande. It dried out considerably revealing a rutted trail of hard-packed red earth, with steeply cambered hard shoulders on both sides. Holding a steady 75mph, the telelever suspension soaked up the bumps. For hours I didn't encounter any other vehicles, allowing me to hunt out the best traction on either side of the road. It was going dusk – always my favourite time on the road. I savoured the emptiness, the cool pure air and the prospect of four months of adventure ahead of my. My only companions were small herds of guanacos and some wild horses.

As night fell, I arrived at an isolated hut-cum-cafeteria and a cluster of trucks and cars. This was Bahia Azul, the port for the Argentinean mainland. The cars were packed to the gunnels with rucksacks, sleeping bags and cooking utensils. There were over 1500 miles of sparsely populated terrain between here and Buenos Aires – these people were prepared for every eventuality.

Not having the luxury of a warm car, I paced up and down the dilapidated scout hut that masqueraded as a departure lounge. I resisted the temptation of a stale bread roll and a cup of instant Camp coffee. Gazing out of the picture window onto a vista of blackness punctuated by a pinprick of light as the solitary ferry headed back, I reflected that I would have to ride some very rough roads through the pitch darkness, with the added risk of vicunas in the road.

We boarded the old tub of a ferry. I remonstrated with the deck-hands not to park my bike so close behind a car, knowing on the sloping deck the driver would roll back as he disembarked and knock it over. They shrugged and ignored me. The inevitable happened and I ended up with a dented fuel tank from where it had fallen against a winch. After blasting the driver of the car and most of the crew, I rode off into the night in a bad frame of mind.

My mood worsened as I realised I had missed the road for the only petrol station. It's 140 kilometres from where the ferry docks at the tiny hamlet of Punta Delgado until the town of Rio Gallegos, with only one filling station marked on my map. It was still another 70 kilometres to Rio Gallegos, no sign of civilization and only fuel in my tank for another two kilometres.

I came across an isolated border checkpoint. They explained that they had a length of rubber tube but no fuel, advising me to ask each motorist that stopped (about three per hour) if they could spare some gas. The response to this question, if posed in the UK would probably commence with "p" and end in "off". The Argentinians who live in this lonesome corner are more public spirited. It only took an hour to find a donor. The young policeman proffered his hosepipe for me to start sucking (if you know what I mean). I tried to explain diplomatically that the thought of sucking in petrol made me gag and would he mind doing it for me. He happily obliged.

Late into the night, I saw Rio Gallegos illuminated on the featureless horizon. Rio Gallegos isn't exactly a temple to hedonism, just a smallish worthy town with a sprinkling of small hotels.

Even when I'm dead on my feet after a long day's riding I never lose my sense of good value and leap into the first hotel I see, preferring to scour the town for a bargain. I tried to negotiate with the first hotelier. I was getting nowhere when I heard a crash behind me and saw my bike lying on its side, belongings strewn over the road. I had parked it on a steeply cambered verge. I hauled it up using every last ounce of my remaining strength, muttering expletives. With a scraped bike and a dented ego I rode around to a much cheaper hotel, parked, and found a *comedor* bursting at the seams with felt-hatted gauchos and their families tucking into churrascos, the juiciest of thick-cut steaks, washed down with heavily oaked red wines from Mendoza. Having not seen food since the previous day – bar a microwave burger, I gorged myself on *bife a caballo*, a steak topped with a fried egg, chips and salad and a bottle of wine; cost – a fiver. Argentinian beef is so flavoursome and well hung, it could convert a vegan.

I spent the following morning shopping for adhesive to fix my indicator and washing the thick coat of dried mud from my bike. It was a chilly, but beautifully sunny day and I wanted to get on the road.

"What ees you country?" enquired a tweedy middle aged man. "I am wanting speak Eengleesh." I made allowances for his broken English. At least I did until he announced that he was a teacher at the main school in Rio Gallegos – an English teacher at that. I reflected that it would not be difficult to land a teaching job myself in this dull little town. What would life be like? Could I stand the endless buffeting wind across the plateau? Perhaps I might get tired of red meat twice a day, every day – my digestive tract certainly would.

Due to the lack of roads in Patagonia I had to ride due west from Rio Gallegos which is on the east coast of the country. I was heading for Puerto Natales on the west coast of Chile. It's frustrating to spend a day in the saddle and not to end up at a more northerly latitude – shame they can't blast a route through the middle of the country. The plateau of southern Patagonia offers endless miles of uninterrupted vistas punctuated by an occasional *estancia*.

There are roughly 30 Argentineans to every square mile, 87% of whom live in urban areas. In the UK that figure is 613 per square mile. Being used to such population density, my sense of solitude was heightened. One of the novelties of this state of being is the ability to stand in the middle of the road and have a pee, confident in the knowledge that you won't see a mortal soul.

I stopped for lunch at the truck stop of 'La Esperanza' because I liked its name and there was no other stop for 150 kilometres. In the gas station I presented them with a $100 bill which threw them completely. Each customer minutely examined it against the window, adding their opinion of its validity. Leaving them to their debate, I browsed amongst the collection of *mate* drinking vessels available in the shop. *Mate* drinking is habitual in Argentina. The *mate* vessel is a spherical palm-sized gourd from which a tea-like infusion of leaves is drunk via an ornate silver straw. My $100 bill accepted and the offer to sell me a *mate* vessel politely refused, the road beckoned.

150 kilometres may not seem much, but on an unrelenting straight gravel trail that saps all one's concentration it can feel like an eternity. As I approached the Chilean border the terrain became undulating hills and valleys with the majestic snow-capped peaks of the Torres del Paine silhouetted in the distance.

Chapter 4

Hola Boyo!

I crossed the Chilean border control as dusk fell with only a further 20 kilometres to Puerto Natales, my overnight destination. What a great little town! Puerto Natales sits on the Ultimo Esperanza gulf, within striking distance of the Torres del Paine National Park. It's a magnet for Chilean and Argentinean tourists in summer, but out of season as I was, it was deserted. I landed a large double room with lake view at the very comfortable Hotel Costra Australis. Wiped out by the invigorating air, I slept for 13 hours.

The receptionist pointed me in the direction of the 181,414 hectare Torres del Paine National Park. At that size I was hardly likely to miss it. The entrance to the Park is 120 kilometres from the nearest town of Puerto Natales. Inaccessibility like this is never going to encourage the Disneyworld crowd. But then you're never going to have the opportunity of being mauled by a puma in Disneyworld. This thought struck me as I read a poster of "do's & don'ts" if attacked by a puma. "Make yourself bigger" it advised me or "Pretend to be dead". I did not think acting would enter the equation. "Bugger off at great speed" would be my choice. I passed herds of guanacos on the approach to the park. They scattered at the sound of my bike. I wonder if a pride of pumas would have been so co-operative?

The 'Torres del Paine' refers to the towers giving way to the Cuernos del Paine – the horns of Paine. These unusually shaped peaks rise to over 2,600 metres. Apart from an abundance of snow-capped peaks there is a plethora of lakes of great clearness, tinged with aquamarine.

Herds of cattle were rounded up by gauchos. These leathery-faced, poncho-clad characters looked the essence of freedom. Living a life long-forgotten in the so-called civilised world. No fancy pickups and Stetsons for these boys.

In these isolated communities, a fuel stop is always a novel experience. My first fill-up that day was via a large plastic Coca-Cola bottle. Fill-up number two was quite surreal. I stopped at the tiny village of Cerro Castillo on the way back to Puerto Natales. An old woman pointed me in the direction of fuel service, a little prefab bungalow. The owner came to the door. He was a dead ringer for Gerry Dorset, lead singer of the seventies pop group Mungo Jerry, sporting a ridiculous Afro hairdo and mutton chop sideburns. Without uttering a word, he whistled to an attendant gaucho who galloped up from a nearby field, dismounted and disappeared into a little wooden Wendy-hut affair. Still no words were spoken. I was about to ride off in frustration when I saw a snake-like leathery hand emerge from a small hole in the Wendy hut. It was clutching a fuel nozzle!

*   *   *   *

Cerro Castillo is the half-way point on the *Ripio* trail back to Puerto Natales. A vicious wind was threatening to blow me off my bike. My forearms ached as I wrestled my machine. Patagonian winds are legendary and this was no exception. I contemplated spending the night under the stars by the side of the road but endeavoured to push on. I rolled into a dimly lit Puerto Natales late at night, falling into a little clapboard restaurant for a warming *paila de mariscos*, a shellfish stew.

Next morning, with just a little regret, I turned my back on the comforts of Puerto Natales, heading first to Rio Turbio, then the long trail north on Ruta 40, a *ripio* road that dissects the vast lands of Patagonia. What can one say about Ruta 40? Endless big skies punctuated by an occasional hovering bird of prey ... that familiar ribbon of grey limestone chips ... infrequent brushes with human- ity ... a gas station and cafeteria is a major event ... looking forward to seeing another vehicle: they'd wave and flash their lights, reminding me that I belonged to the human race.

Yet away from the road was a microcosm of nature. Each time I stopped at the roadside for a rest I spotted a *zorro rojo* – a red fox – spying on me from a distance, a puma skeleton lying under a bush, a pack of wild horses in the distance. It made me think a lot about the forces of nature, the scale of things and how fragile we are in this great wild world.

After 300 kilometres of this monotony I broke my journey at a

Torres del Paine National Park

remote *estancia*. Having spotted some heavily laden bicycles outside, my curiosity was aroused. Brad and Carter are identical twins, looking remarkably like Kieffer Sutherland, though one of them (I forget which) had considerably fewer teeth. They were cycling all the way up to their home in Seattle, Washington equipped with not much more than a pair of saddlebags and a jumbo bag of granola. They were taking three years over their ride and had recently been joined by a young Argentinean. Spending so much time together, the twins had reached a high level of concomitance, speaking in tandem in their calm, gentle manner. They had been seasoned by the road – nothing could faze or surprise them now.

A young Argentinean brother and sister of strikingly Aryan appearance were house-sitting the *estancia* for their uncle. We all sat around the big pine kitchen table exchanging travel stories, enjoying the warmth from the big wood burning range. Brad and Carter shared out their home-made bread. If I were planning a three-year cycling odyssey, I don't think bread-baking equipment would be on my list of essentials. It tasted doubtful too. We hung out, played with their pet sheep, who didn't seem to mind being tossed around like a dog or cat, and finally said our goodbyes. I promised to look up their folks in Seattle.

I rode into the somnolent little village of Tres Lagos as darkness

A romantic interlude in Patagonia

fell. I could not see one lake, let alone three. Tres Casas would be more appropriate. I headed for the only *comedor* in town, ate a reasonable escalope of pork and negotiated with the rather gruff grandmother for a room for the night. Her mood had not improved by the morning. She prepared my breakfast in-between throwing long sighs. Though her wrinkled face beamed beatifically when I crossed her palm with $15.

There was no confusion with exchange rates in Argentina. The peso was linked to the US dollar at the time in a set ratio of 2:1. After some significant growing pains, Argentina had the third highest GDP in Latin American and by far the highest per capita income, though my old lady in Tres Lagos did not look as though she was getting much access to it.

I had a decision to make. Do I continue the 320 kilometres to the next gas station in the hope that my fuel will last out, or do I take a 72 kilometre diversion to a village where there's guaranteed fuel? I go for the 320 kilometre option but don't feel wildly optimistic. 320 kilometres is the absolute maximum I can get out of a full tank. I can't afford any mishaps.

I feel as though I've made a grave error. The first 100 kilometres of road are terrible *ripio* – practically boulders of limestone. I'm getting a lot of wheelspin which is dropping my fuel consumption alarmingly. 200 kilometres and it's little better. After 300 kilometres I'm getting seriously worried. It's just barren desert; I have-

Gaucho, southern Patagonia

n't seen any human life since Tres Lagos and my fuel light has been showing for 60 kilometres. I'm calculating how long I can survive on half a packet of biscuits and 250 mls of water. Will I have to leave the bike with all my belongings and walk the remaining 20 kilometres?

At last – Baja Caracoles! I punch the air with glee. Never have I been so happy to arrive in such a God-forsaken little hamlet. The owner of the gas pump-cum-general store assures me there's fuel at 150 kilometre intervals from here.

I rolled into Perito Moreno in the late afternoon. A dull, single-street town, it didn't make hotel selection a problem – they were all dire. I simply opted for the least dire. The General Belgrano as it was called, deserved a fate similar to the eponymous troop carrier. It was a dark, dank hole in the wall. Fortunately, I was in a buoyant mood having seen a puma cub 20km south of Perito Moreno. I was also cheered by the fact that Perito Moreno was a town – albeit a very boring one – and towns are as rare as hens' teeth in Patagonia.

At this juncture I fancied I had a two-day ride up to Santiago. Wrong! I actually had a five-day-plus ride through the entire spectrum of micro-climates and terrains. I'd miss the bank and the AMEX office in Santiago, leaving me very cash-strapped.

North of Perito Moreno was more desert scrub for at least 200km. The surface was atrocious which slowed my progress significantly. I pulled into an abandoned looking pueblo called Rio Mayo. I tried to get a coffee, failed, and settled for a donut at the local *panaderia* (baker's shop). The sign outside caught my attention: 'Miguel y Nancy Jones'. I had read about the 153 Welsh immigrants who'd settled in this region between 1865 and 1911. They were looking for a better life than that on offer in the Welsh valleys, though God knows why they thought they'd find it in this bleak outpost.

Miguel and Nancy had never seen their spiritual homeland, though they were sent regular bulletins in ancient Welsh from a professor of Welsh Studies at Cardiff University. Although most of the Welsh spoken in Chubert Province has been neglected in favour of Spanish, where it does exist it remains free of modern influence, hence the professor's interest. Nancy proudly showed me her collection of postcards: Colwyn Bay, Aberystwyth, Cardigan ... they were her most prized possessions.

Aside from their preservation of their native tongue, the Welsh community clings to traditions like tea shops, chapel and choirs, plus the sheep look well-satisfied. Miguel, Nancy and family gamely posed for photographs outside their tiny bakery. Nancy thrust a bag of oven-fresh donuts in my hand before waving me off.

As I headed west to join the Camino Austral, the scenery became softer and more fertile. Coihaique is the principal town on the Camino Austral south of Puerto Montt and the point where I joined it. As well as being the administrative capital of the region, it's a centre for outdoor pursuits: hiking, skiing and fishing that take place in this area of natural beauty. Coyhaique reminded me of a budget alpine ski resort. It was the prettiest town I had seen to date, in a contrived sort of way.

What roads! Magnifique! Lovely twisty tarmac roads. Bliss! I forgot my week of bouncing around on boulder trails and savoured the smoothness and quasi-Swiss landscape. My mind wandered to swigging ice-cold pilsner, served by comely frauleins. Then reality kicked in ... the tarmac ended abruptly, we were back to dirt and a night in the dreary little town of Villa Manihuales.

I'm being served lukewarm beer, by a girl (I think) who looks like she should be servicing trucks, in a forlorn little bar the size of the average kitchen. I'm only here because it's marginally better than my depressing little hotel next door. The dormant atmosphere that pervades this town is broken only by the barking and howling of stray dogs and cats that appear to form the majority of the population.

Heading north from Manihuales I soon found out what a combination of dirt road and rain forest spelt ... accidents. The Camino Austral, which will take me the 420 kilometres to Chaiten has only been opened recently, having been carved out of deepest rain forest – the locals joke that it rains 366 days a year in these parts. The road builders simply dug a trail out and did not concern themselves with dressing or tarmacadaming it, leaving a single vehicle width trail of dirt over what appears to be a clay base. The road has a very steep adverse camber on both sides, making it lethal on a motorcycle in the wet – which means ... always. The only place of refuge is the crown of the road on which they'd thoughtfully piled thick gravel. Four-wheel-drive vehicles could handle it, being able to straddle either side of the road, but for a biker it was a nightmare. I now knew why I had not seen a single motorcyclist since leaving Tierra del Fuego.

Fifty kilometres north of Manihuales, my attention was diverted momentarily from the road to a beautiful rock escarpment – I paid the price. The front wheel dug into a thick pile of gravel, I went into an uncontrollable speed wobble as I fought to regain control and CRASH! I dragged myself out of the undergrowth shaken but not too stirred. My bike was lying on its offside on a slope making it impossible to right. I would normally be able to draw on a superhuman reserve of strength but I had only eaten a bag of potato chips in the last 24 hours and my blood sugar was at an all-time low. I just sat in the undergrowth for fifteen minutes, staring disconsolately at my sorry-looking steed. Eventually a pick-up truck drove up. I flagged it down and asked the young couple to give me a hand lifting the bike.

Thirty minutes later the same thing happened again, depositing me in a grassy bog this time. Fortunately, I was able to haul the 250 kilo bike up on my own. I have to find something to eat soon – my low blood sugar is affecting my concentration badly. My riding's not as sharp as usual.

Thankfully, I come across the microscopic 'Communa Puerta

Cisnes' lying forgotten in the mountains. This tranquil hamlet of wooden shacks housed, among others, construction workers. Wisps of smoke trailed from them into the mist-laden atmosphere, promising life ... heat ... food!

I entered a dimly-lit shack of 12ft x 12ft for a breakfast of stale bread and jam and powdered coffee. Everybody was crammed into this tiny room; me having breakfast, the owner washing dishes and some bloke taking a shower behind a partition. A corner of the room was divided off for the road workers' dormitory. It was small, dark and sordid – I shuddered at the thought of staying there.

I slithered down the road for a few more miles before reaching a broken bridge. The only way through is via a stream, the bed of which is boulders and silt. Half-way across my back wheel buried itself in. I'm stranded, immersed to the knees in ice-cold water. I feel extremely pissed off. Trying to power my way out in second gear doesn't help – I just bury myself deeper. There's an acrid smell of burning from the clutch. If I continue I'll fry the clutch plates. After sitting in this ice-cold stream for twenty minutes contemplating my total lack of options, another pick-up turns up and thankfully he's got a towrope. Ironically, I then discover that the bridge probably would have supported the weight of the bike.

I pass the time of day with a couple of Chilean businessmen who run a hare abattoir. They're entertaining a couple of Dutch clients by showing them the rainforest. Thirty minutes later, I meet them coming in the opposite direction. They flag me down to tell me that a bridge 20 kilometres up the road is being blockaded by *pescadores* (fishermen) who are refusing to allow anyone through. Apparently they haven't allowed a single vehicle through for 24 hours. For me to progress north would involve a two-day detour through Argentina. Given the paucity of roads in Patagonia, this was not an option.

The *pescadores* were huddled around a brazier, seeking refuge under a tarpaulin from the omnipresent rain. They looked like they'd walked off the set of the film 'Deliverance'. There's been some serious interbreeding going on in Puyuhuapi, no doubt necessary in a place of such modest population.

I seek out 'El Jefe' (the boss) who seems sympathetic to my plight. I explain I'm due to visit an epilepsy centre in Valparaiso (true) to deliver important medication (untrue) and would they let me through? In the unlikely event that he wanted to see evidence of the medication, I prepared to present the contents of my first-aid kit. Just as he's warming up to the idea, with precision timing I thrust my letter of introduction from the David Lewis Centre into his hand (thoughtfully translated into Spanish) in a bid to clinch it. Unfortunately, he turns to the brain-dead club who easily outvote him. As I see the opportunity wrested from my grip, along comes Alan ...

With a look of the great white hunter in his waistcoat and tan felt fedora, Alan Vesquez is a local hotelier and general entrepreneur to whom El Jefe and his thirty-strong team of half-wits appeared to defer. He spelt out to them the negative impression a foreigner would take away from their country and my unawareness of the political issues surrounding their crusade. They conferred again and hey presto! I was free to proceed. I thanked Alan profusely, though not hanging around too long less they changed their minds.

Chapter 5

Nazis, Pisco Sours and Pony Girls

I struggled along through an ever-deteriorating quagmire to arrive in Puyuhuapi. A small town of 500 people, it is positively urban compared to anything else after Coihaique. It was founded by four Sudeten German families in 1935 from the region of Czechoslovakia annexed by Germany under the Munich Agreement.

After an hour of fruitless banging on doors, enquiring as to the possibility of food in this deathly quiet little burgh, I found myself at the door of a large imposing wooden house with a neatly manicured garden. I had been directed here but felt a little foolish standing there like a drowned rat, my waterproofs covered in thick, glutinous slime.

A stern-looking elderly German lady scrutinised me with disdain, instructed me to remove my filthy outer clothing, but beckoned me in. I was ushered into a dining room where seated around the table was Alan, plus the girl who helped lift my bike from the undergrowth and two middle-aged American women sporting fleeces and sensible haircuts. I joined them halfway through their lunch, slurping down my noodle soup with gusto. The cuisine was traditional German fare: sauerkraut, Wiener schnitzel, strudel. Frau Ludwig allowed her rigid composure to relax and gave a self-satisfied smile each time Alan complimented the food, which was every third mouthful! I cast my eye around the decor of the room; it hinted at a time and place far removed from modern day Chile. I allowed myself to be transported back to wartime Germany. There were faded black and white photos of a handsome young man in an S.S. uniform. This was obviously Frau Ludwig's late husband. It made the hairs on the back of my neck stand up.

The two American ladies who were on a walking holiday looked very politically correct. I wondered what they though of the possible secrets held by their hostess?

After a few more hours of slithering and near misses I pulled up at the small town of La Junta, population 736. I was utterly wasted, yet had only ridden about 100 miles since leaving Manihuales that morning and now it was pitch black, such are the demands of the Camino Austral. Nonetheless, I had savoured the channels, fjords, islands and mountains that border the Austral. To peer through Alerce trees, some of which are thousands of years old, onto a steely vast fjord cloaked in mist is a thrill not to be missed.

Riding into La Junta, the left side of the road was primarily prefabricated construction workers' dormitories. On the right I spotted a hotel called 'Tiempo y Espacio' (Time and Space). I knew this to be Alan's hotel so prepared myself for our third chance encounter of the day.

I was mobbed by a pack of huskies, crossbred with some obscure Turkish strain. Alan called them off: "Ah, my friend, you eventually made it," he beamed. "Welcome to the best place in town," which, compared to a prefab dormitory, it certainly was. Anna, my good Samaritan from that morning, was sitting in the lounge. In such a desolate land with only one road, one has a habit of bumping into the same faces again and again.

After a supper of scrambled eggs we chatted and sank a few Piscos, a very agreeable local spirit, most commonly drunk in Pisco Sours with lemon juice. They told me that there is no continual road beyond Chaiten which is 100 kilometres north, due to the heavily fragmented coastline. I would have to take a $100 ferry ride from Chaiten to Puerto Montt, taking eleven hours.

Chaiten is less than 100 kilometres from La Junta, yet still it took the best part of the day. I stopped to feed some piglets that were grazing in the road. Amazing to think: the Panamericana – *the* arterial road running through the world's most vehicle-orientated continent should have families of pigs roaming it.

Chaiten is another windswept ghost town – or so it seems. I bought my ticket for the Transmarchilay ferry and dived into an elevated wooden *comedor* for a satisfying *congrio y papas fritas* (conger eel and chips). Alan had recommended Mi Casa, a pleasant hotel on a hillock overlooking the Corcovado Bay. Don Federico, the owner, greeted me like a long-lost friend. A balding, middle-aged bachelor, the love of his life was his antique BMW motorcycle, which was in a state of partial restoration. I could not understand where he intended to use it. A street bike on these filthy roads was worse than useless. Still, with year-round rain it gave him something to tinker with. This was only the second motorcycle I had seen in 2,200 miles of riding.

Federico and his ageing mother ran the hotel, which had a lived-in, comfy feel – full of overstuffed sofas and mis-matched chairs. He gave me a detailed account of his life in this rain-sodden region. Although I understood the attraction of such majestic scenery, I challenged the appeal of year-round rain and living in a permanent mudbath. "Ah, but there are special peoples and wonderful types of food to enjoy," he told me, referring to the Mapuche Indians, many of whom live on the Island of Chiloe, a short ferry ride from Chaiten.

With Mauricio Gotelli, service manager of Williamson Balfour Motors

Federico 'phoned ahead to Williamson Balfour, the BMW dealer in Santiago to pre-book my service and first change of tyres. After inviting me to have breakfast with him in his kitchen, he presented me with a fine old bottle of Pisco as a leaving gift. He didn't get to see many like-minded individuals and had adopted me as his pal. He was very hospitable.

The rusting hulk of the Transmarchilay ferry sat in the narrow harbour; its great jaws open to receive its cargo which was predominantly trucks, battered white pick-ups and one lone English motorcyclist. I had reserved a reclining seat which was ripped and filthy. The ferry's PA system cranked out an endless medley of Abba cover versions – I could see it was going to be a very long eleven hours. Traditional Chilean music is wonderful. Why did we have to listen to this crap?

We picked up some more passengers at an isolated settlement along the coast. From the animation and activity it looked as though the arrival of the boat was the highlight of the week – a window to the outside world. The fishermen in their heavy wool sweaters, flat caps and weather-beaten faces look similar to Hebridean Islanders, save for the unmistakable signs of Mapuche bloodlines.

A school of dolphins escorted us out of the bay, their grey, shiny bodies merging with the leaden skies and ice-cold waters. At the end of our journey, we docked at Puerto Montt at 7.30 p.m. I was feeling restless and raring to go. To minimise the 1,016 kilometre stretch from Schlepp to Santiago I decided to put 100 kilometres under my belt and stay at Osorno.

I had been warned that the road to Osorno was heavily policed, being a notoriously fast road. The Carabinieros rarely issue on-the-spot fines – too open to corruption. Instead, they withhold your drivers' licence for four days until your appearance in front of some kind of kangaroo court.

I spotted some Carabinieros in a lay-by twenty miles out of town. An officer was flashing his torch at me to pull over. I had been gunning the big twin for all it was worth and knew a speeding ticket was in the offing. I tore past him watching him gesticulate wildly out of the corner of my eye. Did I want to spend four days in Osorno waiting for the return of my licence? Answer: No! I hoped he had not radioed ahead for support. Fortunately, he hadn't.

It was late at night when I stumbled into a great little four-star hotel, the 'Rayantis'. I enjoyed a gratifying *ceviche de pescado* – raw fish marinated in lemon juice, washed down with some ice-cold crystal Pilsners in the cafeteria, in the company of the entire Osorno football squad. In fact, I was the only diner not sporting a natty emerald green shell-suit.

Osorno was bathed in a warm 'good to be alive' sun on the Sunday morning as I navigated my way out of town. Hordes of young girls paraded in their white frilly Sunday-best clutching little bunches of flowers. They obviously shared the same Mothering Sunday as the USA.

I stopped a mother and flower-clutching daughter for directions "Vas a la iglesia en Inglaterra?" she fired at me, eager to know if I was a churchgoer in England. I admitted I was one of the weddings-and-funerals-only-school. I tried to explain that being C of E in England was generally regarded as a bit of a sop compared to full-blown Catholicism. I had only wanted directions!

*   *   *   *

For the first 150 kilometres or so, the scenery was reminiscent of France – almost like the Loire. Soft pasture, meandering rivers, cows. I was in Chile's lake district but really had not the time to go looking for lakes – I was on a mission for Santiago. The landscape became mountainous, though not on the scale of Patagonia.

A police car attached itself to me. As I slowed down he slowed down, as I accelerated he accelerated. After ten kilometres of this I grew impatient and stopped to ask him what his problem was; "Usted esta conduciendo demasiado lente," he informed me – "You are driving too slowly". Well, I'd never been accused of that before. I promised to burn some rubber from thereon. I had the impression he had been baiting me.

I diverted from the highway to find some lunch in the glamorously-named Los Angeles. It lost nothing in pizazz to its eponymous Californian relative that $50 billion couldn't cure. Everything was shut so I had lunch at the Y.P.F. petrol station. These government-run filling stations offer Les Routiers type restaurants for the not-too-discriminating motorist.

I gazed miserably at the pounding rain bouncing off the station forecourt trying to find all sorts of reasons not to face a tedious 300-mile slog in this weather. As darkness fell, so did a thick blanket of fog. I was in the low-lying central valley, my senses impaired apart from savouring the scent of grapes fermenting in oak barrels. This is one of Chile's foremost wine-producing regions. With visibility down to a few feet I stayed within sight of a juggernaut's tail lights. Without their guidance I would probably have ridden into a field.

At 550 miles I'd ridden enough and searched out the town of Talca, just off the Panamericana. I checked into a gloomy, old-fashioned little hotel, its semi-ornate interior hinted at better days. The manager, an obsequious bespectacled little man fawned over me. I suspected I was the hotel's only guest. He hovered around me, wringing his hands Uriah Heep like. "Would Señor care for anything?" A bit of personal space would be nice, I mused.

I settled down on my bed with a stale ham sandwich and a putrid instant coffee to watch some television. My guidebook had nothing much to say about Talca, even though it was the most important town for hundreds of kilometres. Realising that Talca, fog and Sunday evenings are a hopeless combination, I channel surfed until I came across 'UK Raw' an English cable programme that showed great promise. It was the only English programme I had seen in South America. It featured two naked women wearing full bridle, saddle and muzzle ... the lot. They were being 'ridden' by two men who frequently beat their bare bottoms with riding crops to which they responded with neighing noises. This was followed by a feature on 'S & M Morris Dancing'. I was beginning to understand why Latins find the English difficult to fathom.

Chapter 6

Smog and Stardom

The air pollution enveloped me like a blanket as I rode through the outskirts of Santiago. Factories appeared to produce little more than noxious smoke. My eyes itched and streamed. I slipped into the maelstrom of buses spewing their diesel smoke on the Avenida O'Higgins and glimpsed a sign-post to Liga Chilena Contra de Epilepsia. Great! This was the epilepsy centre I had intended to visit and I had stumbled across it without a problem.

I parked up on a pretty side street outside a smartly discreet low-level building. A dapper middle-aged man came out to greet me. I explained my David Lewis Epilepsy Centre fundraising crusade in minute detail. He introduced himself as one of the directors of the Centre and whisked me inside to meet his colleagues. Past a phalanx of white-coated pharmacists dispensing drugs and into a separate administration block behind where I was ushered into the office of their head of PR, Cecilia Campos. She briefed me on the objectives of five Chilean epilepsy centres and four medication dispensaries. I enquired if there was any way I could help "spread their word". Yes, if I could come to her office the following day she had set up a couple of interviews with the national press. I called the BMW dealer, postponed my service and tyre change and made it a date.

The long-distance biker always faces a number of chores when he arrives in a new town. There's kit to clean, laundry, boots to repair, bike to wash – not to mention the endless writing of letters, faxes and diary entries. It's always a good way to familiarise oneself with a city. I busied myself with these tasks for the remainder of the day. Having reached my first major city I decided to have a blow-out that night and treated myself to a fine French restaurant. I decided to give the conger eel a rest tonight. I stayed in the old centre, avoiding the expensive northern suburbs of Las Condes and

Providencia. Ironically, the hotel that Cecilia recommended to me was the very one I had stayed in a fortnight previously, when I had flown into Santiago.

Sex sells in Santiago. It does in most parts of the world but it's more noticeable here. There are some great little espresso bars, though you might think you'd wandered into a lap-dancing club by the skimpy attire of the waitresses. Walking past a shop, I noticed a life-sized cardboard cut-out of a naked girl in the window. Nothing unusual in that ... except they were promoting wheelchairs and prosthetics!

I had wandered into the pedestrianised zone that dissects Avenida O'Higgins. It was thronged with people, as you might expect in a city of over five million inhabitants; chatting, browsing, hustling businessmen looking preoccupied, dashing to meetings, expostulating into mobile phones – it could almost be Western Europe, except for Mapuche Indian families congregated on their rugs, swathed in bold primary colours selling trinkets, advocating greater liberty for their people by silent protest or, quite simply, begging. Chile, like all Latin American countries, is a coming-together of ancient and modern beliefs.

After liberating some funds from the ornate and exquisitely beautiful 'Banco de Chile' I hiked out to the suburban sprawl of Providencia from the AMEX office. I never like to travel in any developing country (though Chile is more developed than most) with anything in excess of US$1,000 on my person. I had to try and predict my needs at two- to three-weekly intervals and fax my mother to wire out sums of money, to be collected at pre-determined banks. The presence of an AMEX office allowed me to top-up any shortfall on my card.

Back at the Liga Chilena, a press conference had been set up. The President and Vice-President of the Liga were in attendance along with a bunch of photographers and a journalist from 'El Diario', Chile's national daily tabloid. I find speaking lucidly into a hand-held microphone hard enough in English, but in Spanish ...

I rode over to Las Condes to drop my bike off at the BMW dealer, Williamson Balfour, for a service and much-needed new tyres. Las Condas was an education in how the other one percent of Santiago lived in this pristine neighbourhood, some 15 kilometres from the old centre. Gleaming pickups, malls and expensively coiffeured women made me feel as though I were back in Wilmslow. Even the

$900 bill for my service and tyres was reassuringly expensive though even Wilmslonians would balk at an invoice like that.

Back at the hotel, I met up with Mary Ann Jones, who'd been introduced to me by one of my clients, Anna Meadmore. Anna, a professional mezzo-soprano had met Mary Ann during a two-year stint at music college in London. This was immediately prior to the '73 military coup in Santiago, which we glossed over as much as is possible. I wanted to give her the opportunity to sing her country's praises, not dwell on its darker periods. With her short no-nonsense snow-white hair and impeccable Received Pronunciation, Mary Ann was more Chelsea than Chile. After an hour of quaffing Pisco Sours with Mary Ann, I rooted out a baroque-style restaurant for the ubiquitous *ceviche y congrio*, served by white-jacketed old retainers. It had the sort of old-world charm that only exists in the memories of the British.

It did not take me long to find a copy of 'La Cuarta' the following day. While strolling down Avenida Brasil and its dusty old colonial-style side streets, watching the street corner banker, reading the cries for liberty from the graffiti artists, peering into the endless car spares shops (not that I really needed a gearbox for a '92 Daewoo), I bumped into a familiar figure: ME! My photo was plastered over the window of a news kiosk ... and the next... and the next one. And so it went on all day. I stopped for a haircut. The peluquero (hairdresser) recognised me instantly from the paper, which made the cut progress at a snail's pace while he and his assistants fired questions at me. The only person's questions I was eager to answer were from the rather comely junior. Unfortunately, she never asked any. I was beginning to experience the 'David Beckham effect' of instant recognition: fame, but no fortune in this case.

That night I dined at 'Los Buenos Muchachos', a cavernous restaurant with a floor show, but not *that* type of floorshow, which is just as well, as I would not be enjoying too many lap dancers, having left my wallet back at the hotel. This was embarrassing, given that I had long since given my order. Fortunately, the manager took me on trust, though they obviously decided to compound my embarrassment by sitting me at a little table by the stage and placing a Union flag on it with 'Inglaterra' emblazoned across it. Thankfully, they didn't hand me a knotted handkerchief to wear for the duration of the evening. The floorshow featured a bunch of dancers dressed as *campesinos* (peasants), to the accompaniment of Chilean folk songs. They danced the 'cueca', a courting dance which involves the wafting of handkerchiefs in the air. This was followed by a troupe of Mapuche Indians, convulsing their semi-naked bodies to the sounds from the elongated 'trutruca' horn and the 'kultrun' drum. An enjoyable spectacle.

I had to go back to Williamson Balfour before heading north. I was not happy with the way the bike was idling and wanted a couple of other things checking before tackling the Atacama desert. I was just about to leave when a call came through from Cecilia at the *Liga Chilena*. "Canal 1 have seen your article. They want to interview you live this evening for '¿Por Qué lo Pasó?'. Can you come down now?" I was desperate to make up some ground, but the lure of appearing on Chilean TV's main prime-time show was just too great. I was sitting in Cecilia's office before she could say "¿Por Qué lo Pasó?".

Cecilia introduced me to a lissome young girl who was to interview me while the film crew set up for an outside broadcast. My mouth felt dry. The interviewer was to fire off some questions to me, while I had a linkup to the studio through an earpiece. The prospect of a three-way conversation in an unfamiliar language was daunting, but thankfully it was a knockabout, fun interview that did not require searching answers.

I returned to the Hotel Conde Ansurez for a *third* stay. It was beginning to feel like 'Groundhog Day'. Yet another venerable Santiago restaurant for dinner, its tobacco-stained walls playing host to faded photos of long-forgotten Chilean luminaries who had patronised it over the last century. *Congrio* in *ceviche* this time – is there no end to the versatility of the conger eel?

I was sad to leave Santiago. I bid a fond farewell to Bernarda, the receptionist at the Conde Ansurez, who had been following my exploits with great interest, and roared off.

Chapter 7

The Atacama Desert: life in a lifeless land

Hugging the coast on Ruta 5 North, I felt a considerable dip in temperature. The rugged coastline was my constant companion. I saw a whale break cover briefly and slap the surface with its vast tail, but apart from that, it was a sparsely populated and repetitious coastline. But the salty tang of the air was refreshing. I lunched on a sizzling skillet of ... yes – *congrio*! *Caldilo de congrio*, a kind of half-stew, half-soup, *must* have been the only interpretation of an eel I had not tried.

Fuel stops were becoming scarce, forcing me to knock on someone's front door to see if they had any spare supplies. The ubiquitous sawn-off plastic Coke bottle was produced, saving the day.

Giving a live interview for Canal 7, a Chilean TV station

A monotonous road through mountainous scrubland and sporadic small cacti eventually brought me out to the pleasant and seemingly affluent coastal seaside town of La Serena. At 473 kilometres north of Santiago, I didn't expect recognition in this remote outpost, so was surprised when a group of middle-aged men approached me who were able to tell me exactly what I was up to, having read about or seen me on TV. I found a fifties-style wooden-clad motel near the Plaza de Armas run by a humourless man who issued me with a long list of what I could and could not do in his establishment. I did not even bother broaching the subject of a discount.

The market place in La Serena is the focal point of its community. Around a pretty little church, artisans and trinket sellers offer their wares to weekend visitors and tourists, though at 946 kilometres round trip I could not see many Santiagans saying "Oh, let's just nip up to La Serena for a couple of days". The streets running off the Plaza bore the names of Arturo Pratt (Chile's greatest general) and Bernardo O'Higgins (its greatest liberator). I had noticed that just about every town in Chile bore the name of these two legends on its streets.

I had to wander around the town's archaeological museum pausing at a rather disturbing Atacamenos Indian who had been remarkably preserved in the ultra-arid Atacama desert for hundreds of years. The lack of deterioration in his skin tissue was a testimony to the zero rainfall in 400 years in parts of the Atacama and the absence of pretty much any living thing.

The Atacama Desert was my next big challenge. I had a vision of the curator of the museum in a hundred years time, leaning over the shrivelled corpse of Ashley Rhodes and explaining to an enthralled group of Japanese tourists: "Yes, here's a particularly well-preserved example of a male of northern European origin. We found him in the Atacama desert next to his motorcycle, which we assume ran out of petrol". This occurrence is probably number four in my mother's ten worst-case scenarios, somewhere between inadvertently taking a dip in a piranha-filled river and being robbed and gang-raped by tequila-crazed Mexican 'perros locos'. I made a mental note to buy a jerry can.

La Serena's air of sophistication was not matched by its restaurants. The ersatz Lebanese restaurant I dined in was of the opinion that people in the Lebanon ate nothing but rice. It was like a re-run of the Monty Python Spam sketch, but substituted by rice. Every time I wanted anything I would have to bawl across the empty restaurant at the waiter who was engrossed in watching cartoons on TV. His lack of desire to serve me and general lethargy was forgotten only at bill-paying time.

Knowing it was unwise to venture into the Atacama without a map that indicated fuel stops, I waited for the Automovil Club de Chile to open. Strangely, the door was unlocked yet there was not a soul in the place. I hung around for an hour to no avail. I tried a travel agent: nothing. A petrol station perhaps? Well, they could offer me a dozen different flavours of in-car air freshener, but nothing so rudimentary as a map. I began to realise that any four-wheeler would just fill up at every fuel stop, but being on a motorcycle with a 320-kilometre range I simply *had* to know their locations. I had been told that 300 kilometres was the normal distance between gas stations in the Atacama. This was a game of Russian roulette.

The road climbs steeply away from the coast, north of La Serena. Normally I would have swept past the long lines of ancient diesel-spewing trucks grinding their way up the steep mountain pass, but the long sheer drop to my offside made me feel vertiginous.

I stopped for a can of soda and a flaccid sandwich at a remote truck stop. Some teenagers are hanging around, joking with a plump girl in the cafeteria. What on earth do they do for fun? It's about 700 kilometres to Antofagasta which is the next major town. The tedium must be unbearable. I'm amazed nobody's run amok with an Uzi, at the end of their tether.

The desert is endless – a ribbon of tarmac through hours of nothingness. There isn't even the ritual of cleaning bugs off my visor to perform. Nothing seems to live here – not even insects. My only diversion is an occasional makeshift shrine at the side of the road – normally a small pile of rubble with a little cross and maybe a plastic effigy of the Virgin Mary. I assume there's someone buried under these crude affairs. Life (what there is of it) must be so harsh and monotonous out here that death is a seamless extension – hence the lack of fuss.

I come across a more permanent-looking shrine, fenced in, with a child-sized icon of the Virgin Mary. A couple of hundred licence plates and plaques from buses and trucks adorn the fence. This is

Independence Day parade in Caldera

obviously a shrine to commercial drivers who have met their maker in the Atacama. A figure appears, almost magically, from behind the shrine. It's a dog – almost skeletal and on the verge of starvation. It's trying to eat a piece of tissue paper. My heart went out to this pitiful creature. It must have been abandoned. I try to find a suitable vessel to give it some of my water, with no success. I attempt to pour water into its mouth from my bottle, but it's too frightened to come near me. It strikes me that water or food would only prolong its miserable existence for another few days. The kindest thing anybody could do is to shoot it. I ride off with a cloud of depression hanging over me.

By late afternoon I'm back on the coast again and riding around the streets of the modest little port of Caldera, which serves as a terminal for the loading of iron ore. It makes for a welcome oasis from the desert. I was feeling upbeat at the prospect of mingling with humans again. Caldera enjoys a little tourism, but at this time of year was as dead as the proverbial dodo. I found a little hotel which only had one guest – me.

There was not much to do, but find a little telephone office and book a call to England. But that was all to change ... because here I met Italo.

*   *   *   *

Italo was a construction worker, building some homes about five kilometres out into the desert. These would house miners who worked the vast copper and nitrate mines throughout Atacama. A friendly streetwise guy in his thirties, he introduced me first to his boss, a pure-blooded Peruvian Indian, and another younger colleague who hailed from Iquique, further north. They invited me to have dinner with them in a simple parilla (grill room). I offered to pay for the wine, which the waiter explained was all 'unavailable', despite the fact that twenty different wines were listed. He did have *one* in stock. Not unsurprisingly, it was the dearest one on the list. We adjourned to the beach, picking up an extremely cheap plastic bottle of wine. The four of us gazed out into the dark mass of the Pacific. I'm not sure whether it was the wine (which tasted like a by-product from the nitrate mines) or the sombre ocean, but my new-found friends became very maudlin for their homes, wives and girlfriends. They talked wistfully of Santiago, Iquique ... of good times spent away from the bleak wilderness of Atacama. I, on the other hand, was happy to be in this nothing little town, luxuriating in the knowledge that I had three and a half months of adventures in front of me. Later, amidst a lot of hand-shaking and back-slapping, I bade farewell to my new friends. I liked them – they embodied the openness and generosity of spirit that's everywhere in South America.

The soothing, sleep-inducing effects of the best Cabernet Sauvignon in the house had been cancelled out by the second bottle of 50-cent gut rot. I woke up with a storming hangover. It felt like cannons were going off in my head. They were ... 21 of them to be precise, along with bands ... lots of bands: trumpets and percussion, all assailing me through the paper-thin walls of a $15 a night hotel room.

I dragged myself out into the dazzling daylight to witness the spectacle of town dignitaries, families in their Sunday best, uniformed schoolchildren, boy scouts ... everyone and their dog. There actually was a dog – a mangy little black thing – which led the naval band at the head of the procession. The navy-and-white-clad sailors marched in perfect unison, their brass buttons gleamed in the early morning sun. The dog seemed unaware of the long procession behind him – I don't think he was an invited guest.

This day in 1879 Chile gained control of the northern deserts from Bolivia and Peru. It's hard to see what any country would want with these arid wastes, but the area was rich in nitrates, much of which lay in Bolivian and Peruvian land. Chile mined most of the nitrates as part of Anglo-Chilean alliances and felt justified in claiming the land for itself, culminating in the War of the Pacific from 1879 to 1883. The people of Cordera were clearly proud to be Chilean. The size of the parade was in stark contrast to the modest size of the town.

Schoolboys in white shirts and navy ties clambered all over my bike, eager to have their photo taken. Their angelic-looking sisters, dressed uniformly in navy blue smock dresses, were much more coy, standing well back and collapsing into fits of embarrassed giggling whenever I spoke to them.

I rode on to Chanaral, the last town before the 400-kilometre stretch to Antofagasta. I ate a delicious *paila marinara* in a gas station cafeteria, asking myself why in Britain we're reduced to flaccid cheeseburgers in styrofoam containers, when service station food *could* be this good. Nonetheless, the rest of Chanaral doesn't stand up to close scrutiny. Its wooden houses perched on a hillside overlooking the mouth of the Rio Salado looked sad and dilapidated. It had the feel of an oasis which was exactly what it was – the last sign of civilisation, bar another small town, for 400 kilometres.

Chapter 8

Drunken Midgets and Dirty Habits – Arica to La Paz

As I drew nearer to Antofagasta I watched the sun go down and felt the temperature plummet in a matter of minutes. Although the temperature in 'Anto' never drops below 10^0 centigrade, being on the coast, the inland desert is a different matter, regularly reaching minus 10^0 centigrade. There was a biting wind blowing and nowhere to hide from it. I swaddled myself in whatever clothing I could lay my hands on.

Antofagasta is a truly bizarre town. Large industrial and mining operations dominate the approach giving it an eerie other-worldly feel. There's little to indicate one's arrival in town – unusual for a town of almost 230,000 inhabitants. Sat on its own at the city limits facing the ocean, I spotted the Carrera Club Hotel – a glitzy newly built luxury hotel. I figured I could use some luxury after the Atacama.

I presented myself in the marble foyer looking like Mad Max but with more grime and less attitude. Out of season it was a steal at $63. I bounced up and down on the king-sized bed like an excited child. Luxury is so much more rewarding when its been hard-earned.

I'd met a Canadian mining engineer back in Punta Arenas called Rob Sedgemore. He lived and worked in Antofagasta so I looked him up. Ten minutes later he was outside my hotel in his white pickup. Things had not worked out too well in Canada for Rob; with a divorce behind him in Canada, he had temporarily turned his back on his homeland and sought his fortune in the Atacama where he had spent the last four years.

Sunday nights aren't too exciting in Antofagasta so he took me along to the home of some of his Canadian colleagues who were having a barbecue. They shared a small white stucco villa in a nondescript side street.

Rob ushered me into a dimly lit room. Two bodies were hunched over computer games, totally absorbed and oblivious to our presence. Rob introduced them, they grunted in return. I stood there addressing the thinning pate of a ginger-haired, thirty-something who only expressed enthusiasm when he had annihilated a few dozen intergalactic invaders. We drank fizzy American beer and stood around in the kitchen while they talked in-talk about the mining industry and memorable nights spent in the fleshpots of 'Anto'. Other Canadians drifted in and out of the house in the course of the evening – all looking as though they'd just crawled out of bed. The pork chops and beans were good. I wolfed them down while the assembled diners belched and farted in approval, pausing occasionally between mouthfuls to scratch their groins or straining bellies. "Hey man, we were in Arica last weekend – boy, were we partyin'! I was like wasted," (pauses for belch) "and, boy, you wanna see ass? Get to Arica!" says tall ultra-dishevelled younger man to balding ginger nut. "Yeah, right," grunts the latter.

The only relief in this sea of testosterone were half a dozen slim, pretty Chilean girls sat in the adjacent room chatting animatedly between themselves. I discovered that they were the 'girlfriends' of the Canadians. I wondered what such attractive charming girls could find to admire in these Neanderthals. I was witnessing the stark reality of the power of the greenback.

From Antofagasta I headed in the general direction of Bolivia which first involved an 850-kilometre slog to the northern border town of Arica. The Canadians had issued dire warnings about street crime in Bolivia: "Hey man, they'll rob your ass, and don't even *think* about using credit cards – you'll go home to a bill like a third-world debt!" But, nonetheless, I was looking forward to it.

There's a choice of two routes from Antofagasta to Arica; the Panamericana runs inland through the desert, the alternative coast road is equally barren but has the added attraction of the breaking Pacific to one's left, plus the attractive coastal town of Iquique two-thirds of the way up to Arica. It seemed a good lunch stop.

Iquique is derived from the Aymara word 'Ique-Ique', meaning place of tranquillity. After the War of the Pacific it became the main centre for nitrate trade. Today it trades in tax-free consumer goods with a vast free zone selling every imported item imaginable.

The sun was beating down as I rode into town, though a gentle coastal breeze made life much more tolerable. I stopped to watch a travelling circus pack up but could not stand to watch tigers in cages too small for them to even turn around. Lunch cheered me up – on the patio of the Yacht Club, looking out to the ocean. I looked predictably out of place, sweating in my leathers amongst besuited Atacaman businessmen, but was nonetheless treated very cordially by the waiter who recognised me from TV!

I felt relaxed and contented gazing out to the Pacific with a belly full of mariscos and Chilean Sauvignon Blanc. I had decided to indulge myself, food-wise, over the next two days, as Bolivia was likely to be an exercise in culinary deprivation. It would be nice to stay in Iquique I thought, lounging on the beach at Cavancha watching the crashing surf (Iquique has the best surfing in Chile) but I knew I had to make Arica.

I had been on the road for almost ten hours that day. I still had two hours to go when night fell like a black cloak. I was concentrating hard – the mountain pass was twisting and tortuous, giving way on my offside to a sheer drop of many hundreds of feet into a vast canyon. The mountainside blocked out any natural light there was, the road was narrow and roughly surfaced. Giant trucks thundered towards me – I squeezed past them with inches to spare. Would there by any wild or domestic animals wandering in the road? All I needed was to have to swerve for an errant llama; there was no crash barrier at the edge of the road – I'd be a gonner.

I urged myself on in my fatigued state in the knowledge that fewer overnight stays in dead-end towns meant longer stays in interesting places, and La Paz, Bolivia's capital, was likely to be one of these.

The mountain levelled out. Vast quarries and nitrate mines dominated the landscape. Huge diggers toiled away, sending clouds of blinding, choking dust in their wake. These yellow behemoths had caterpillar tracks taller than me – and I'm tall!

*   *   *   *

110 kilometres south of Arica I stopped for a Coke at an improvised truck stop. It was very late; I needed to press on but the thick dust and treacherous road were demoralising me. My mindset wasn't right. As a biker, I can identify how a day is likely to pan out. Some days my riding flows beautifully – a

seamless merging, a unity of man and machine. This was not one of those days.

Despite its slightly temporary frontier town feel, Arica isn't bad for a border town. I found a nice, modern little hotel hidden away in a quiet back street. The owner seemed to think that although I had ridden the 4,700 miles to Arica without getting lost, I might struggle to find my way to the restaurant round the corner. He provided me with the services of the proprietress of the Chinese restaurant next door to escort me.

After sitting in a cavernous restaurant as the sole diner, I felt in need of some action. It was to be my last night in Chile after four weeks of riding, and I was ready to sink a few Cristal Pilseners. There was a luridly painted first-floor bar adjacent to the restaurant, euphemistically called a French Bar which in a town like this could have all manner of connotations. It was a surprisingly pleasant little cocktail bar, full of dark inglenooks but not a bargirl in sight. It was part-run by Amanda, the epitome of Englishness in a fluffy little twinset. She had come a long way from High Wycombe to be with her Chilean boyfriend. He dealt with the daily running of the place, she charmed the customers.

On this occasion she was politely listening to the maudlin outpourings of a diminutive Indian perched on a barstool next to me. He grinned a toothless grin at me, called up another Rusty Nail and cerveza chaser, and continued to utter incoherent statements of love and devotion to Amanda: "You, Eenglees lady are my special friend! I think you beautiful lady ... " and suchlike. I watched his little squat body lean at a precarious angle. He looked in grave danger of falling and even at only 5' 2" it was a long way down. He fixed me with a stupid grin, gold inlays flashing. Fingering the many gold rope chains around his neck with bejewelled digits, he announced to me: "Me very rich man. Me big man in Arica" (though obviously not in the literal sense). At which point he promptly fell off his stool, collapsing in an untidy heap at my feet. There was no alternative but for Amanda and me to carry him down the steps and deposit him on the street. It made a strange sight – a tall, willowy English rose and an even taller Englishman frog-marching this diminutive drug dealer (I took that to be his occupation) out of the bar.

*   *   *   *

Before leaving Arica, I phoned ahead to the British Embassy in La Paz. Marie-Elena, who handles PR for the Embassy, booked me a meeting with the head of neurology at the general hospital. He dealt with all matters relating to epilepsy and would clearly benefit from some media attention. I was to meet with him the following morning.

The climb out of Arica into the Cordillera gains height at a very rapid rate. It's 4,000 metres up to the vast plateau of the Altiplano, with La Paz lying in a depression within the Altiplano, of about 370 metres. I had the foresight to fill my jerrycan in Arica – it's a six-hour ride with no gas stations, up steep, twisting, fuel-sapping inclines commandeered by white-knuckled Bolivian truckers who give road space to no man.

Snow-capped volcanoes pierced the sky, just some of the highlights of the stunning Lauca National Park, along with the serene lakes of Chungara and Cotacotani. Llamas and vicunas grazed at the side of the road. I savoured the stillness on the shore of Lago Chungara, miles away from the belching exhausts and grinding gears of the trans-Andean truckers. Marvelling at the uniformity of the volcanoes, breathing in the thin, dry mountain air, I felt at peace. I heard the unmistakable thrum of two four-stroke motorcycle engines and saw two dots grow larger on the horizon. As they drew nearer, I made out luggage, spare tyres and aluminium panniers like my own. These were long-distance bikers. Dutch ones to be precise – a submarine captain and his wife on Yamaha Teneres.

They told me they were circumnavigating the world, over five years. They had only one year left of their adventure and were mentally preparing to re-assimilate into 'normal' society. They had nuggets of information for me about crossing the Darien gap from Colombia to Panama, though after regaling me with horror stories of two weeks spent trying to liberate their machines from Panamanian Customs I decided they just had not greased enough palms, and I would have to try it my way.

We rode together up to Bolivian immigration at the lonely outpost of Charana. Whilst queuing for stamps and chatting, I was aware of the piercing stares from five bowler-hatted and beady-eyed indigenous Indian ladies. They were sat on the earth floor in a row, like the Five Stooges. Their multicoloured voluminous skirts splayed out on the baked earth. Their faces never

Near the Chilean/Bolivian border

betrayed any emotion – dislike, animation, curiosity, interest ... nothing. I watched them draw wads of grubby boliviano banknotes from under their skirts – they were the official currency changers. When that transaction was over, *empanadas* (pastries) and other 'platos tipicos' were extracted from the even deeper recesses of their skirts and offered to us. I was very hungry but also mindful of the passage that Che Guevera had written in his motorcycle diaries about the tendency of Indian women to use their skirts on themselves and their children in lieu of toilet paper. He went on to describe the skirts of Indian women (particularly those with lots of children) as "veritable warehouses of excrement". It may come as no surprise that I gave the *empanadas* a miss.

The light was failing as I rode a dead straight road across the Altiplano. Desperately poor *campesinos* were toiling on the unyielding land, trying to eke out a miserable existence with the assistance of their half-starved mules.

About 66% of Bolivians are pure-blooded Indians. They are loosely divided between the 'collas' from the Altiplano, and the lowlanders, known as 'cambas'. The collas certainly get the rougher deal: their only respite from the drudgery of their lives is in the form of wads of coca that they masticate. This offers a mild buzz to lift the spirits slightly and acts as a hunger suppressant. Hunger is their constant companion.

One has to ride with caution at night on the Altiplano; not only are there the inevitable stray dogs and other assorted animals roaming the roads, but the Indians have very bizarre sleeping arrangements. They like to sleep with their heads and torsos on the road to avoid mosquitos (not that there can be too many of these at 4,000 metres) leaving themselves open to instant decapitation!

Chapter 9

Life in a Bolivian Prison

Nothing prepared me for the approach to La Paz. It's as if one's falling off the edge of the world and there, lying at the bottom of a steep canyon, is the world's highest capital city. I approached it through the teeming adjacent city of El Alto, which lies around the rim of the depression. This area is almost exclusively inhabited by indigenous people – a veritable sea of bowler hats, or 'bombins' as they are called locally.

As I reached the bottom of the canyon and the district which roughly acts as its epicentre, I was caught up in a manic surge of traffic; little white minibuses serving as 'colectivos' swarmed like ants, beaten-up taxis and every other form of shit-slinging decrepit old heap, all funnelling down steep narrow streets that simply could not absorb them. The fumes and cacophony of horns were oppressive to say the least. My bike was running like an old dog, with the oil temperature climbing steadily to worrying levels. Being an air-cooled flat twin, it did not seem to like the thin air or lack of forward motion.

I fancied staying at the President, the world's highest five-star hotel, but settled for something far more prosaic across the road. I noticed that the people I came into contact with in the tourist industry: hotel staff, bank officials, shopworkers, etc., would almost exclusively be 'Mestizos' (mixed race) whereas the pure-blooded indigenous peoples would be engaged in seemingly fruitless enterprises like selling items that nobody really needed from one-man stalls on street corners. This seemed a sad state of affairs, though, despite the lack of social inclusion, there doesn't appear to be any obvious resentment between the haves and have-nots.

I had a very late dinner in the hotel. I wanted to get the lie of the land before eating in any dodgy places in La Paz. Several seasoned Latin American travellers had told me that La Paz was the only city where they'd picked up food poisoning. They probably weren't carrying my armoury of preventative medicine.

I awoke the following morning experiencing the other unpleasant legacy of a stay in La Paz, *mal de altura* – altitude sickness. I had a constantly nagging headache. I hit the street. I wanted to sit down and have a cup of tea after only walking a few metres. My legs felt like lead, my breathing was laboured, my head felt detached from my body. The only symptom of *mal de altura* I was not suffering from (thankfully) was flatulence.

I walked across town to the general hospital where I was to meet with Dr De la Q ... I never found out what the Q stood for. An urbane, white-coated man in the autumn of his years, Dr Federico introduced me to his two colleagues and Craig Cottrell, a young Englishman who freelanced for the Bolivian Times, a somewhat thin weekly paper aimed at Bolivia's English speaking expatriate community – not that there are too many of those. I discussed the work of the David Lewis Centre with them and gave an interview for the paper. The British Embassy had arranged for a film crew to come down to the hospital for an outside broadcast. This interview by Canal 2 was to be broadcast nationally that day. In the meantime, Canal 7, another national channel, had invited me down to the studio to do a live, on the couch 'Richard and Judy' style interview. The svelte, pelmet-skirted interviewer rattled questions off to me while I tried to divert my gaze from her legs and remember my verb endings. I was slotted in between a lady giving a demonstration of very intricate needlework and another discussing counselling techniques.

Using the bike to get around La Paz was not a good idea. The streets are way too narrow, preventing the possibility of 'filtering', road signs are scarce and taxis cheap and plentiful. I walked instead, gasping for breath, up to the Museo de la Coca. The museum reflects the history, medical value, cultural and political significance of the coca plant. I had already discovered the second attribute for myself and was taking regular cups of *mate de coca* to combat my altitude sickness. A Dutch backpacker introduced me to *pastilles de coca*, a coca-impregnated sweet. They're sold for two bolivianos per sweet and supposedly make one feel more vibrant and enhance respiration. The cultivation and chewing of the coca leaf is perfectly legal in Bolivia. It's mainly grown in the tropical lowlands of the Chapara region by some 25,000 families. It came as no surprise to learn that almost all of it is refined into cocaine before starting the long trail north to 'Gringolandia'.

*   *   *   *

I had arranged to pick up some money in La Paz, wired to me from England. Presenting myself at the door of a ridiculously opulent (in view of the state of the national economy) glass and steel edifice, I was frisked by machine gun toting guards, asked to surrender my passport and, in the dizzy heights of the top floor, was introduced to an 'official' who further minutely inspected my documents. He told me to come back in two hours after my money had been 'obtained'. I enquired as to why Banco Central de Bolivia, Bolivia's most prestigious bank, could not lay its hands instantly on 750 lousy bucks which had been ordered and paid for two weeks previously. No response was forthcoming.

I spent my available two hours in a similarly frustrating bid to liberate a couple of hundred dollars from my American Express card. It took the full mind-numbing two hours and several calls to other AMEX offices in the UK, USA and Mexico, of all places. Hmm ... not bad ... half a day to draw £600.

It's not a widely advertised fact (not by the Bolivian Tourist Board, at any rate) that it's possible to take a guided 'tour' round the San Pedro Prison. Not being a fan of conventional tourism, I gravitated towards the idea. I had asked around and was told to simply turn up at the prison gates and ask for Freddy. I arrived at the prison gates feeling somewhat uneasy. This was not an educational visit to some long-gone jail where objects or incarceration become merely historical curiosities. This was the real thing – a working prison in the year 2000 and a Latin American one at that, to give it a suitably desperado feel. It certainly looked very old. Would this have been the kind of joint Butch Cassidy and the Sundance Kid would have wound up in had the Bolivian army not decided to shoot them instead? I tentatively entered a dank, bare stone-walled holding room. Hatchet-faced, swarthy guards frisked me and searched my daysack. They took my camera (but missed the miniature one at the bottom), took my passport, wrote my passport number on my arm, rubber stamped my arm a couple of times and passed me on to the sniffer dog. A hand-written entry card was proffered in exchange for my valuables. I began to feel uneasy about the $900 stuffed into my money belt. Looking over the guard's shoulder, I saw a large iron-grilled gate that separated me from a living nightmare. Hordes of restless, semi-deranged prisoners were clutching the gate and yelling through it to me: "Hey, gringo! Give me dinero!" and similar inviting greetings.

A fair-skinned hulk of a man with a large football head came forward. I took this to be Freddy. He led me through the gates. I was alarmed to find that Freddy was a serving prisoner, not a guard as I had expected. Dozens of hands grabbed me while I literally clutched Freddy's arm. Realising I spoke Spanish, Freddy deposited me temporarily with his 'boss' to whom I paid my fee. He was from Uruguay and had got caught smuggling cocaine out of Bolivia – rather a lot of it judging by his lengthy sentence. I was passed back and forth between the two of them. The Uruguayan looked preoccupied – his eyes darted everywhere, veins stood out in his forehead and neck. He looked to be high on coke. He would habitually take a wad of dollar bills from his pocket and count them – probably advisable when you're living with half the pickpocket population of Bolivia. Yet I sensed a presence about him – like nobody would trifle with him. This was one mean hombre. I was not wrong: Freddy cheerfully announced to me later in the tour that our Uruguayan friend had murdered a couple of the inmates, including the previous 'top dog'.

The prison is open-plan: murderers, rapists, petty thieves all co-exist – to a point. Those with money can bribe the guards for an 'upgrade' to a roomier cell. The going rate is about US$1,000. Needless to say, the Uruguayan had a very commodious cell. Drugs, contraband and prostitutes, along with improved food, can be purchased from the guards. There is little sense of order or control. The losers are the dirt-poor Aymara Indians. They can't afford an upgrade and are forced to live in the most cramped and squalid inhuman conditions. I practically gagged when I saw the revolting kitchen where their food was being prepared.

The strangest thing about San Pedro is that wives, girlfriends and children are allowed to enter freely and even stay the night if they wish, though God knows why they would want to. I passed the tiny cell of an Aymara Indian. His whole family was in there, presenting him with a little birthday cake. It greatly moved me.

Freddy abandoned me for ten minutes while I waited to regain entry into the holding room. The guards did not seem in any hurry to let me in. It was the longest ten minutes of my life!

*   *   *   *

Back at the hotel I took a long, hot shower to remove the 'smell of the nick'. Freedom never tasted so good. I had met a girl earlier in the day who part-owned a small travel agents. Elisabeth and I had arranged to meet that evening for dinner. She walked me around the streets of the old centre, pointing out things of interest while I quietly froze. The temperature in La Paz drops radically at night. I didn't want to turn up for a date in a fully armoured Dainese motorcycle jacket, so faced the consequences of travelling light. We ate in a restaurant called 'Gringo Limon'. I was the token gringo.

I always like to keep an eye open for interesting keepsakes or souvenirs but drew the line at one of La Paz's offerings (after the poncho and woolly hat, that is). I could not see myself digging in my bag when I returned and presenting my mother with a dried llama foetus. "Mum, this is just what you need to fend of evil spirits. Why don't you pop it there by that Capo di Monte figurine?"

Elisabeth took me out with her friends that night. We congregated in the kind of bar that tourists never seem to find, played some dice, and adjourned to a disco/karaoke joint where we sang along to a mixture of South American and Mexican love songs, mingled with obscure 70s hits by Tina Charles. A vast quantity of El Ince, a dark stout-type beer was drunk. Foolishly, I accepted a lift home in the jeep of one of Elisabeth's friends. He was barely capable of standing. Most of the journey was completed on the sidewalk with occasional detours onto the road.

My hangover seemed exacerbated by the altitude, but I couldn't afford to write the day off. If I were to make it to Cuzco in Peru by the end of the following day I would have to leave town. Elisabeth came to the hotel to give me a couple of tapes of Mexican and Bolivian ballads, pose for some photos and wave me off.

Climbing out of the city to El Alto, I had a choice of two routes. I made the mistake of asking a couple of *campesinos* for directions. Generally, Latin American men will send you in any direction rather than admitting they don't know. They want to please you. Well, it didn't please me very much when I was sent on a 140-mile

"Imagine how you would like your hair" says the advertisement

wild goose chase, causing me to lose the option of a night in Puno, which was still another four hours away.

After some dismal far-flung suburbs I found myself hugging the banks of Lake Titicaca, the world's highest navigable lake. In the long shadows of the late afternoon I sat on the patio of a makeshift restaurant, looking out onto the ocean-like grandeur of the lake, eating freshly caught barbecued trout. A nice white burgundy would have slid down well, but there was only one alcoholic drink on offer; beer in huge brown bottles, the quality of which was implied by its ridiculously low cost.

Despite the rapidly disappearing light and livestock-strewn roads, I decided to push on to Copacabana, where I might find accommodation in something other than an adobe hut.

The road ground to an abrupt halt. Separating me from food, beer and bed were the Straits of Tiquina. A naval rating in full whites approached me to sell me a ticket for the necessary raft crossing. Being approached by a *bona fide* member of the national navy in a country that doesn't even have a coastline may seem strange, but I knew that Bolivia was the only land-locked country in the world with its own navy, so I stumped up my bolivianos.

The vessel I was invited to board was a crude raft of

strapped-together logs. I carefully navigated the bike on, making sure to avoid the huge gaps between the logs, not an easy task with a laden weight of over 250 kilograms. The setting sun behind the mountains, the perfect stillness of the cool evening and the gentle swishing of the raft made it a euphoric ride. This all came to an abrupt end when I tried to disembark. The dead weight of the bike collapsed on me. My £200 Dainese full-race gloves were about to be swallowed up by Lake Titicaca. With the help of another two passengers, I eventually managed to drag the bike ashore.

A snaking mountain trail pointed me towards Copacabana. The stars shone with outstanding brilliance in the inky sky – at this altitude I felt as though I could almost touch them. Copacabana is a pleasing little town, inhabited almost exclusively by indigenous Indians with the odd gringo backpacker 'gone native' in poncho and woolly hat with flapping earpieces.

I found a cheap hostel which did not invite lingering – the staff were sullen and uncommunicative – so I took a walk around town, pausing to watch a *peña* folk band performing in the market for late night produce shoppers. The chill night mountain air was filled with the percussion beat of the *caja* drum and the unique sound of the *charango*, Bolivia's traditional miniature guitar. Grilled trout from the lake was pretty much the sole dining option, so I had it for supper too. It's good – firm and fleshy with a greying tinge that suggests wild rather than farmed.

Being of interest to gringos, Copacabana's many cafés make an attempt at reproducing the 'American breakfast'. All sorts of exotic imported items are advertised: waffles, yogurt, scrambled eggs, etc. I parked myself in a spartan little café in the main plaza. "Yes, I'll have yogurt with granola, eggs over easy with wheat toast and an espresso, please," I ordered from the well-upholstered Indian lady who seemed to be performing all roles. "Yogurt no hay," she replied curtly. "O.K. I'll stick with the eggs and toast." "No los tenemos," came the answer. "Well, coffee sounds good – do you have it?" I ventured. "Hmmph ..." She waddled off to the kitchen and came back with a chipped cup of hot water and a sachet of Nescafé which, from the taste of it, had never known a Nestlé production plant. Never mind, there was a lovely clear blue sky, the good people of Copacabana were assembling outside the delightful Moorish cathedral that dominated the plaza and ... what was the long line of vehicles doing at the entrance to the church? I watched in fascination as the local Padre sprinkled holy water over the air filter of an old Chevy S-10 pickup. A serious-faced Indian couple were watching in earnest, clutching bouquets of white flowers. All the other vehicles were bedecked in flowers. I considered lining my bike up for a blessing, but not being the world's most regular churchgoer, felt a little hypocritical.

*   *   *   *

The 'road' from Copacabana that took me the short distance to the Peruvian border was something of a nightmare. I hit a patch of deep sand at one point, went into a huge speed wobble and almost took out a *campesina* and her donkey.

Peruvian Customs were predictably slow. A gaggle of nine-year-old *tramitadores* surrounded me. These youngsters latch themselves on to you at almost all Latin American borders. Their job is to expedite the bureaucratic process that is mind-boggling in its tedium and complexity. It isn't made any easier when new 'fees' are introduced. I find the best way to test their legitimacy is to point-blank refuse to pay them and to start quoting imaginary names in Government, Consuls, whatever. If the official in question doesn't take a stance on it, then it's a safe bet that he's tried to dupe you. As I left Bolivia to enter Peru, I experienced the unofficial tax 'sting' from the moustachioed immigration official. I steadfastly refused to pay it and walked out of the immigration hut, leaving him muttering darkly

Chapter 10

From Inca Heaven to Highway Hell

Peru is a 'Pais con Futura' (country with a future), or so said the numerous placards I passed within minutes of leaving Bolivia. It was the eve of the national elections with Fujimori trying to hold on to his presidency for another term against a challenge from ex-shoeshine boy, Alejandro Toledo. That's a meritocracy for you.

Though my initial impression of Peru was not greatly different to that of Bolivia, it has to be admired for its hillsides of neatly terraced crops. It's a veritable garden of Eden in the more hospitable climes, prompting the Government to spearhead a return to self-sufficiency farming, not seen since Inca times.

I stopped at an open-air market for a photo opportunity. Within minutes I was surrounded by hordes of people. A few brazen ones would question me, but the others just stared awkwardly. I singled out one particular bowler-hatted lady for a photo with the bike. I thought she looked rather sweet – at least I did until she put a finger to the side of her nose and evacuated the contents of her left nostril at my feet.

Puno, the next major town, was going to be too near for an overnight stay, but there was not much on offer between that and Cusco, so I braced myself for the five-hour haul. The towns I rode through were reminiscent of Malaysia or India, hundreds of bicycle-driven rickshaws clogged the streets performing death-defying manoeuvres exceeded only in their stupidity by the motorists. It is said that the wearing of a hat is the infallible badge of the bad driver. Nearly every driver in Peru wears a hat!

I thanked God I was on a tarmacadam road (of sorts). It was pitch black, with numerous long stretches of road dug up for repairs. I stopped at a roadside bar – a prefabricated hut with the grand total of eleven bottles of beverage, all of them 'Inca Kola'. "Er, I think I'll have an Inca Kola," I ventured to the unsmiling, stout Indian lady behind the bar. She handed me my first ever bottle of Peru's national soft drink. I had seen it advertised on every available plac-ard throughout the country, at least, on those not extolling the virtues of 'Peru – Pais Con Futura'. It's a honey-coloured concoc-tion, fairly sickly and won't cause any loss of sleep in the Coca-Cola boardroom.

I rolled into Cusco very late at night, immediately charmed by its narrow cobbled streets and fine colonial architecture. The Hotel Savoy is a short walk from the Plaza de Armas, which I hoped would guarantee a better room rate in this fairly expensive town. It's a faded fifties establishment with cavernous rooms and an equally huge sitting room with some riveting magazines on display like 'Norwegian Pipe Line Journal' and a stack of titles alluding to such fascinating subjects as nuclear fission – written in German to boot. I settled down for a read with a limp sandwich and instant coffee before dozing off on the settee in a crumpled pile of fly-spattered Gore-Tex.

I had arranged with a tour guide, operating from the street, that I would be collected at 5.30 a.m. that morning to be taken on a heli-copter ride over Machu Picchu, the famous lost city of the Incas and the sacred valley. It was an extravagance but with the limited time I had available it was the quickest and best way of viewing these magnificent sites. Having set my alarm for 4.45 am and feel-ing like death, I was somewhat irritated when my guide did not show up. However, in a city of 275,000 where every second person appears to be a tour guide, finding a replacement was not difficult.

I ended up paying a ludicrous amount to take the train up to Machu Picchu. There is no road, not even one navigable by bike, from Cusco, so I allowed myself to be 'processed' by the cartel of guides and tour operators that transport people to this much-visited world heritage site. I was annoyed, knowing that had I been around for longer I could have found an alternative way up. I was sure the Indian traders didn't pay $70 return and wished I could have shopped around rather than coughing up like an obedi-ent gringo punter. Nonetheless, I boarded the rickety old train at 7.30 a.m. for the three-and-a-half-hour climb up to Machu Picchu.

Initially, the ancient locomotive climbed almost vertically, shunting back and forth on its narrow gauge track, rocking violently until it found its level. There were no local people on this train, just pink-fleshed gringos in denim cut-offs and running shoes. A sea of Ray-Bans and baseball caps.

Shortly after Ollantaytambo the train juddered to a halt. Dozens of small brown hands, women's and children's, thrust huge corn on the cobs through the open windows of the train. They looked like giant marrows in size, studded with polished golden nuggets of corn the size of grapes.

*   *   *   *

I certainly had not expected to enter the lost city of the Incas through a turnstile, but that's exactly what we did, having been decanted from our coaches that took us the last stretch from the railway station to the entrance. But any reservations I had were dispelled by the awesome peak of Huayna Picchu, the mountain that overlooks the site.

Machu Picchu is a complete Inca city in an impressive state of preservation. The Incas built Cusco and Machu Picchu about 900 years ago. Not only did they display impressive masonry skills (their buildings are constructed to the most exacting specifications) but they operated a very sophisticated form of government based on a religious and secular hierarchy that ruled over the 'Ayllu' as the village community was known. They clearly believed in a meritocracy though and would invite talented individuals to join the ruling elite. The ruling class deferred to Sapa Inca who was the vice-regent of the Sun God that they worshipped.

Machu Picchu was abandoned in the 16th century and was gradually reclaimed by the jungle. Some 400 years later in 1911 an American, Hiram Bingham, stumbled across it, closely followed by a team of archaeologists from Yale. Today, Machu Picchu is one of the most visited archaeological sites in the world, having come to particular prominence in the last 20 years. I don't normally care for organised tours but Machu Picchu is a 'must do'.

*   *   *   *

Sitting in the Inca Grill on the Plaza de Armas that night, I learnt that while I had been dead to the world the previous night there'd been a mini revolution right there in the Plaza, a stone's throw from my hotel room. A crowd of young people had launched a protest against alleged political corruption endemic to President Fujimori's party. In the best traditions of South American democracy and freedom of speech, the police simply waded in with their riot batons. This debacle proved inconvenient to me – the police had banned the consumption of alcohol in the town centre for the next couple of nights. After a day of trudging around Machu Picchu I had been looking forward to sinking a couple. The proprietor of the restaurant had worked out a solution. He gave me my *vino tinto* in a cup and saucer.

The other diners were almost exclusively tourists. There seemed to be a problem in the kitchen and most meals were being sent back. This provoked an interaction between the diners along the lines of: "God, this is awful – what's yours like?" I had an exchange with two American girls about their respective steaks. It's fair to say that these native Floridians were experiencing a degree of culture shock. They regaled me with tales of twenty-hour bus rides on decrepit buses, 'personal hygiene issues' and various other areas of dissatisfaction. I gently pointed out to them – particularly Paula Beth who was more damning than her colleague, Deborah – that they may have been happier in Disneyworld, and to try and keep a more open mind. Nonetheless, they were great fun. We enjoyed the band playing their 'quena' pipes, had a bunch of photos taken around the town and arranged to meet up in a few days time in Lima, which would be the next major port of call for the three of us.

I had had a dispute with Juan, who had arranged my Machu Picchu tour, over the final balance owed. I realised he was not going to back down when he drove down to my hotel at 7.00 a.m. to "have breakfast" with me. He was so tenacious about the $20 in dispute that I thought he might chain himself to my bike. I examined my conscience and decided to pay up.

I was pleased to pick up some reasonable tarmac riding out of Cusco. There was the usual menagerie wandering around the road but, nonetheless, an enjoyable morning passing through interesting rustic pueblos. I soon learnt never to take things for granted in Peru, the road abruptly turned into a rutted cart track of unbelievable awfulness. No signs existed. The odd Indian *campesino* I stopped did not speak Spanish or even want to try. There were so many cattle, mules and pigs wandering in the road that I could have got the body count into double figures. I managed to keep it down to just one close call with a hen.

I tried to get up into third gear and weight the footpegs, but each time I gained speed and consequently better traction, a goat or some such animal would casually stroll into my path, precipitating a close encounter with the trenches bordering the 'road'. I struggled gamely on in first and second, wrestling the bike's ungainly dead weight, sweating and cursing.

As if by magic the road started to climb and suddenly transformed into a good tarmac mountain pass with some fabulous curves and switchbacks. Savouring the sheer pleasure of great roads, I gunned the boxer twin, late braking for the tight hairpins and cranking it over, footpegs scraping. Even fully laden the Beemer would handle it with aplomb, the telelever front suspension eliminating nose-dive as I braked hard for yet another second-gear hairpin.

It was a biker's dream road. Feeling euphoric, I stopped at an isolated village to buy a freshly-squeezed mango juice from a roadside vendor. The usual gaggle of interested villagers gathered around, asking questions and peering at the bike. I amiably answered their probing questions, enjoying the fresh mountain air and the warmth of the sun, when, suddenly, I felt a perceptible shift in their questioning: where did I keep my money? And how much did I carry on me? A shifty looking youth was trying to persuade me to enter a dark hut to "look at a gold detector". Older, more sinister-looking men gathered round. I felt the hair stand up on the back of my neck. I had given away too much information too freely, lulled into a false sense of security. I knew the 'Sendero Luminoso', the Maoist guerilla group known elsewhere as the Shining Path, had been very active in this region, and I was sensitive to the fact that, while not particularly active at the moment, they had not become model citizens overnight. Trying to maintain my eye contact, I ever-so-casually turned the ignition key to the start position and clicked the gear shifter down into first. Even the plump middle-aged woman who'd sold the mango juice to me was studying me with heightened curiosity. I seized the opportunity as a small gap appeared in the crowd. I pressed the starter button, engaged clutch and disappeared in a cloud of dust, helmet hanging from my arm, juice thrown to one side.

As I got back on the mountain pass and checked that I was not being followed, my breathing returned to normal, though I still felt uneasy. I knew another five minutes in that place and I would most likely be handing over my worldly possessions at the end of a gun.

I've developed an inherent ability to separate regular situations from potentially dangerous ones – that one had clearly been the latter.

I banked the bike over for a sharp right-hander, partially obscured by a low bridge parapet: disaster! A thick carpet of loose sand was hidden from view by the parapet. I hit it at about 45 mph with the bike cranked right over. I watched the bike gracefully slither down the road on its side with me rolling along just behind. After a few metres we both came to a halt in an untidy bundle. After a cursory check of my major limbs I attempted to drag the bike towards safety at the edge of the road, aided by a young sheep farmer who'd pulled up in a tiny hatchback, full to capacity with live sheep.

We inspected the damage under the gaze of a dozen unblinking sheep. I was OK, other than a large rip in the knee of my leather jeans. Thanks to the crash bars, the bike had only suffered a super-ficial grazing but the bad news was the right-hand aluminium pannier. The side had been ripped open like a tin of sardines, though thankfully, the pannier rails seemed undamaged. We forced it back into some kind of shape, which would hopefully suffice until I could get it welded in Lima.

I felt as though I had had enough aggravation for one day, but knew it was only just beginning, the road turned into rubble again. I had see a town on my map which looked to be very close. I would enquire how long it would take: "Ocho horas, Señor". Eight hours. I would usually deduct a couple of hours from their estimates based on the knowledge that they'd probably only ever made the journey on a pre-war antediluvian bus with a llama on their lap. However, in this case they were not wrong. The road deteriorated further, gouged by giant caterpillar tracks engaged in some futile recon-struction programme. A median of large, sharp limestone rocks was bordered by huge mudbanks. I took a couple of low-speed tumbles – it was just proving impossible to stay upright. After tack-ling one huge mountain in this condition, I eventually came to a small dusty village. Decrepit old trucks were grinding down the main street leaving a wake of dust and noxious diesel fumes. Precariously loaded with limestone boulders, I mused that it would not be difficult for one of those boulders to fall on my bonce if I were to ride too close to them.

I found an unappetising cafeteria with a gang of ragged street children gathered outside. After administering various coins to ensure the security of the bike, I walked in to be greeted by the proprietor, an unshaven tousle-haired ruffian. His T-shirt completed the picture: grubby, sweaty and with "FUCK YOU!" emblazoned across the front in bold red letters. In fairness, it had probably come via an aid worker. I would frequently come across elderly Indian ladies in remote hill villages sporting 'Microsoft' or 'Tampa Bay Rowdies' T-shirts. I felt sure that they had not the slightest idea of the meaning of either.

The trail followed a deep gorge. The scenery was great, but I was choking on dust, my clothing covered in a thick white crust of lime-stone dust. Sweat poured off me as I stood on the footpegs, pounding away, trying to tame the best by keeping the momentum going. The bars were writhing. I tried to make steering corrections through pressing my weight on either footpeg, backed by gentle counter-steering. My concentration was heightened by the prospect of losing control and plummeting 50 metres into the gorge that lay a mere metre to my right. This went on for five long hours until nightfall. Within minutes it was pitch black. I was utterly exhausted, with the prospect of another two hours of riding to the small town of Charlhuanca. I miraculously got through two bogs, managing to keep the bike upright – just – the back wheel slithering wildly from side to side. I lost control a couple more times; on the second occasion, too beat to drag the bike up, I just left it on its side with the lights on, right in the middle of the road while I sat on a boulder and contemplated it, waiting for another vehicle to show up and give me a hand.

Late that night, I limped into Charlhuanca, which not unsurprisingly was a dark, depressing little town. There were two hotels. I opted for the better of the two – it cost me the princely sum of £3 a night. When I saw the room, I felt that I had been ripped off – I had seen better cells at San Pedro prison. Bathing facilities were a communal standpipe and, God, did I need to bathe. I decided to investigate the miserable little *comedor* next door. The one thing that had spurred me on that day was the prospect of a juicy steak and a bottle of *tinto*. I gazed miserably at the two bony trout with their heads still on, their lifeless eyes looking up at me. They seemed to be laughing at me: "Ha ... go home gringo!" I felt depressed and exhausted in equal measures

I fell asleep over my meal, head slumped on the table. I was gently woken by a sweet-looking Quechua Indian girl who looked about 14 years old. Elena was a bright girl; she was, in fact, 19 and planning to move to Lima to attend University. I felt sorry for her, trapped in these dire circumstances, working in her parents' depressing little eatery morning, noon and night. She was pretty and full of youthful vitality. She needed a life that Charlhuanca could not give her. I retired to my cell and slept a fitful sleep in all my clothes, anxious to have no contact with my filthy flea-ridden mattress.

My biggest problem on this trip was getting on the road nice and early each day. I did not have that problem in Charlhuanca. I was accelerating out of town at 5.50 a.m., eager to put distance between myself and my previous night.

Chapter 11

Inca Kola and
Teenage Infatuation – Peru

The road to Piquio gained altitude very quickly. I went from a slightly tropical climate to bitterly cold freezing fog, all in the space of an hour. My helmet visor froze over, stalactites of ice hanging off its edge. I stopped to drag on layers of outer clothing – anything to combat the cold, even to the extent of donning two woollen neckwarmers and a balaclava. I was still shivering uncontrollably despite my Michelin man appearance but within an hour, I dropped a couple of thousand metres in altitude and was sweltering. The local village idiot at the last village had given me wildly inaccurate information about the next fuel stop, and so I descended a mountain on a wing and a prayer, trying to wring every last drop of juice from the petrol tank. I finally ground to a halt just a few metres short of a fuel pump. The owner could not change my high denomination bill, so I had to wait there for another hour for more customers to supplement her float.

The road eventually connected with the Panamericana at Nasca, where I pulled into 'El Campo' for lunch, a roadside palm-fronded eatery with a pool adjacent – an unusual sight in these parts. Xaviero, the owner, leaped out of the pool to greet me. Looking every inch like Freddie Mercury he gave me a beatific smile and pumped my hand vigorously. "Welcome, my friend! Why don't you join us in the pool?" I surveyed the pool which was noticeably all-male, inhabited by muscular young men. I politely declined and opted for a fillet of pork and chips instead. Xaviero brought a young man over to introduce to me: "Dis ees Meester Brian, my special friend!" exclaimed Xaviero. 'Meester Brian' looked a little uncomfortable. As Xaviero wandered off to watch his 'pool boys' Brian told me his story. He was an Irish backpacker travelling all over the Andes and had all his worldly belongings stolen the previous day at the bus station in Lima. Xaviero had witnessed the theft and offered to put Brian up free of charge until he could get some money wired out from his family in Ireland. What seemed like a good idea at the time was quickly losing its appeal as Brian realised what the pay-off might be.

Back on the Panamericana, which by now was a poker-straight desert highway, I came across the famous Nasca Lines, a collection of lines, geometrical shapes and even drawings of animals carved into the desert. They are believed to have been etched by three groups of people: the Paracas, the Nascas and the Ayacucho, ranging from 900BC to about AD630. Best seen from the air, the symbols are thought to represent a huge astronomical pre-Inca calendar. There are, however, various other theories abounding ranging from one claiming that the ancient Nasca people were balloonists, evidenced by the presence of some balloon imagery on ancient tapestries and a rather more realistic view that they were the tracks of running contests. As tourist attractions go, spending 50 bucks on a helicopter ride to see a number of ruts would not be high on my list of priorities.

The Panamericana stretched on for hours, nothing but endless scrub with the odd little oasis, the boredom alleviated by the odd 'Inca Kola' billboard. As night fell quickly I had to keep my wits about me. My previously clear visor had become slightly opaque, so I had to wear my tinted visor even at night – changing the darkness to pitch black, with huge trucks rumbling along just inches from me. I arrived at a police roadblock where three cones had been laid out to divert traffic. I asked the attendant policeman which route to follow for Lima. Seizing his opportunity, he tried to fine me for 'crossing the cones'. While he minutely examined my documents I made the decision that the best line of defence was counter-attack. I announced that I was a visiting police official (he probably couldn't read the English in my passport and wouldn't know a hairdresser from a haematologist) and was appalled at the fact that the cones had not been illuminated and that insufficient signage was evident. I would have to make a formal complaint to his superior, asking him "And who would that be?" Deciding that I was a genuine case (or a complete nutter) he let me go.

The outskirts of Lima, with their seething cauldron of traffic, are chaotic. After getting lost a few times and, at one point, having policemen jumping out at me, shouting and flashing torches in my face (I later discovered that certain 'fast track' expressways are forbidden to motorcyclists) I arrived at the Swissotel, determined to savour some five-star luxury after my previous night of deprivation. As I walked into the lobby, filthy, unshaven, hollow-eyed and looking like an extra from 'Mad Max', a hundred immaculately coiffured heads swivelled round and regarded me with a mix of curiosity and not a little disdain. The staff, however, hid their feelings admirably. Although I could not negotiate the rate of $165 any lower they very kindly phoned around for a cheaper deal, finally settling on the four-star Hotel Alcala del Rio in the pleasant suburb of San Isidro, a relative snip at $60.

I had a list of tasks the following day: I needed my aluminium pannier welded and beaten out, leather jeans repaired and reproofed, collect my money drop, do laundry, repair boots and finally ... get a haircut. The hotel fixed me up with a driver for the day, and whilst Wilfredo was expensive (clearly visible from his brand new Hyundai, crisp shirt, tie and blow-dried barnet) he proved to be a huge help, ensuring that everywhere I went I got the best deal and service. He dropped me in the old colonial centre, where I ate my best-ever *ceviche*; this platter of raw fish and crustaceans had, as usual, been marinated in astringent lemon juice – but this time it was served with yucca and sweet potatoes and washed down with dark malt beer, known as maltina.

I took to Lima instantly, despite Patrick Symmes referring to it in his excellent book 'Chasing Che' as "a foul metropolis of dusty brown buildings and clogged streets and cold hills'. I had to admit to liking the place myself, especially the fine colonial architecture of the Plaza Merced, where I spent a contented couple of hours poking around and enjoying banter with the locals, all of whom struck me as friendly and open. Pretty girls paraded around the Plaza in groups, talking and laughing animatedly, while even prettier policewomen, sporting a variation on the white pith helmet, were directing the traffic with gusto. The traffic in Lima is yellow: swarms of yellow VW Beetle taxis in various stages of decrepitude fill the streets with their noxious fumes. They're made under licence in Latin America and aren't renowned for their build quality or low emissions.

The Club is a venerable Lima institution, a gentleman's club that flourished in a time when Lima's heart and soul was to be found around the Plaza de Armas. The wealth has now moved to the health clubs and spas of Miraflores and San Isidro – both prosperous, anodyne suburbs.

I spent an absorbing couple of hours wandering around the five-storied Club de la Union, marvelling at its faded grandeur. I tried to visualise Liman society of 50 years ago, gliding across the maple floor of the grand ballroom to the strains of the moustachioed and brilliantined house band. I tried to imagine the deals that had been cut over the acres of emerald baize that covered the vast tables of the billiards room. Had the details of the War of the Pacific been plotted in this very room? I believed they had. Floor after floor, I explored every nook and cranny of the club. I didn't see a single member of staff. Then I found a tiny wood-panelled cubbyhole of a bar where a solitary white-jacketed waiter fixed me a Pisco Sour. He looked like an old retainer, the last one off the Titanic. After inspecting the huge oil portraits of former presidents hung along the main hallway, I stepped out into the dazzling sunlight and bustle of modern Lima in a melancholic frame of mind.

*   *   *   *

I managed to contact Deborah and Paula Beth, my new-found friends from Cusco. They would not be arriving in Lima for another couple of days. But I needed some further alterations to my offside pannier which might involve some welding, so did not mind the extra delay. I spent the day pleasantly, taking a long lunch in an upmarket Mexican restaurant in Miraflores. The manager and I discussed Peruvian politics. I asked him who he favoured as a future President of Peru. He told me that although Alberto Fujimori is regarded as something of a dictator, the 'people' (I took that as meaning the middle classes) wanted to see a leader who could maintain law and order, however despotic he may be.

I heard a somewhat different viewpoint from Margaret Sanderson that evening. Margaret is another old friend of Anna Meadmore who had introduced me to Mary Ann back in Santiago. She had arrived in Lima after completing her degree in Latin American Studies, some years ago. Over dinner of *ceviche* and pasta (an odd combination), she told me about her work in the Pueblos Jovenes, literally young villages where Lima's poor have gathered: huge, communally run barrios. Margaret's role as a committed Christian was to offer pastoral care and practical help to these unfortunates. Needless to say, she did not share quite the same political viewpoint as the Miraflores restaurateur. She told me over an absorbing three-hour dinner how economic refugees from the impoverished *campo* would arrive at the Pueblos Jovenes which they would treat as a staging post before moving into the city proper. Apparently, a couple of these projects had been applauded as models of self-government.

Deborah and Paula Beth turned up at my hotel the following morning. After a predictably over-the-top Floridian greeting (lots of hugging and general gushing) I got Carlos, Wilfredo's sidekick to run us downtown. First, I wanted them to see the anachronistic Club de la Union for themselves. "Well, it's kinda neat but it sure needs fixin' up," was Paula Beth's verdict. Deborah, usually the more positive of the two, was more enraptured; as a concert pianist she related better to historic buildings. Paula Beth only needed to know how clean their bathrooms were. We adjourned to L'Eau Vie, a French restaurant run by nuns, whose profits went to the poor of Lima. It certainly had a calm, serene atmosphere, allied to the comforting knowledge that nobody's going to massage your bill or short change you. Paula Beth made various references to 'John' during lunch, usually backed up with an affirmation that he was 'communicating' with her at that moment via the spirit world (healing powers and spiritual communication were always on the agenda with Paula Beth and Deborah) and had informed Paula Beth that I was a 'good' person with lots of 'positive energy' around me. After some probing as to who the late 'John' was, she confessed to me in hushed, trembling tones that it was the country singer, John Denver, to whom she had been engaged to be married at the time of the air crash that took his life.

In the cab back to my hotel, Deborah clutched Paula Beth's leg with one hand and the back of my neck (I was in the front) with the other, in order to transfer yet more positive energy to my body. The cab driver was eyeing them suspiciously through his rear-view mirror. He clearly thought he had picked up a couple of gringo weirdos.

Deborah gave us a recital of stunning virtuosity on the hotel's piano while we enjoyed a farewell drink. I'd enjoyed our time together, but now it was 'back to business'.

*   *   *   *

My 548-kilometre haul to the coastal town of Trujillo began in a fairly depressing vein. I had become soft after a few days of four-star comfort and of being a tourist, and had to re-focus my mind as I battled through the slum outskirts of Lima – the usual combination of grimy shacks and geriatric buses that filled my helmet with their suffocating fumes. Roadside vendors lined the streets, peddling everything from rotting fruit to bathroom mirrors. A dense mist enveloped the coastline, the temperature dropped and I clicked into automatic pilot with nothing to stimulate my imagination other than the vast sand dunes that lay to my left. At times like this I would crunch numbers in my mind, computing distances, fuel consumption figures, working out what I had spent, what I was likely to spend ... while all the time the big boxer twin thrummed beneath me. I would sometimes marvel at its ruggedness. In rural parts of Peru gasoline often has an octane rating of only 77 – 18 less than standard unleaded – yet the BMW ran smoothly at all times.

I was distracted from my musings by a sign advertising *Cocina de Lena* outside a roadside eatery. Let me tell you good reader, that if you're ever tempted by Cocina de Lena, give it a miss, unless you enjoy a scrawny pork chop, rice and beans. The only palatable part of the meal was the over-sweet Pisco Sour.

I rode into Trujillo late that evening. Despite unprepossessing outskirts, the Plaza de Armas was rich in fine colonial architecture – similar to Cusco's. Like Cusco, a crowd of disaffected youth was forming in the Plaza de Armas. The tension was palpable, not helped by the heavily armed legions of police and military waiting expectantly.

After checking into the Hotel Libertador on the west side of the Plaza, which would ensure me a ringside seat of any possible post-election riots, I wandered off to find a restaurant. Towards the end of my meal, I suddenly felt very strange. My legs were like lead, heart palpitating I could feel the colour draining from my face. Desperate to get out of the place, I staggered out of the restaurant, crashing into a couple of tables on the way. I steadied myself against the outside wall, taking in huge breaths, trying to force some air into my lungs. My first thought was that I had been drugged – a common practice in Latin America, via food or drink, as a precursor to robbery. I tried in vain to pull myself together, only too aware of my vulnerability in this dimly-lit dodgy-looking backstreet. With one hand steadying me against the wall, I concentrated on putting one leaden leg in front of the other. The occasional person I encountered would cross to the other side of the street, convinced I was a drunk. I could see the Plaza de Armas ... just a few more paces. Staggering into the hotel, I slurred *llave* (key) to the pretty receptionist who I noticed had one hand on the phone, in the event of any unpleasantness. I miraculously found my room and collapsed in a leather-clad heap.

The next morning, I woke up and remained dormant, not wanting to move a muscle in case I collapsed again. Amazingly, I was still alive, with not a clue of what had caused the previous night's trauma. Satisfied that everything was OK, I took it easy, spending the morning watching black-and-white Mexican musicals from my bed, before packing the bike and getting back on the Panamericana, bound for Chiclayo.

I had hoped the stretch north of Trujillo was more inspiring than the 500 kilometres south – sadly not. The road surface was generally good, flanked with the predictable huge sand dunes. Each little hamlet I rode through gave off a nauseating smell of woodsmoke and rotting fish. At intervals of several kilometres there were concrete shelters, though I couldn't work out who or what they were protecting.

There was still a heavy mist, though it was preferable to ride through it in daylight than darkness as I had the previous night. Peruvians, like most Latin Americans, have strange nocturnal driving habits. Anyone (truckers included) will wait until it's completely pitch black before putting their headlights on, and then only ever on full beam in a bid to dazzle oncoming traffic. Their rear lights will usually be inoperative as will one of their headlights, making it impossible to tell a truck from a motorcycle. Cattle trucks and ox carts have no illumination whatsoever and villagers will meander in the middle of the road (often drunk) in the darkest clothing they could lay their hands on, willing you to run over them. The only time vehicles do use their lights is for manic flashing, seemingly when there is no need to do so. At first, I assumed that this was to warn me of lurking police, but they really just want to say "hi".

I stopped in Chiclayo for lunch. After riding around the town looking for a particularly elusive restaurant that had been recommended I gave up and settled for a 1970s-style roast chicken joint called the *Pollo Loco* – 'crazy chicken'. My waitress, Milagro, was one of the most beautiful creatures I've laid eyes on. Her deep limpid eyes were framed with impossibly long blue black eyelashes. Her forearms and cheeks were lightly covered with fine black down. Her slightly chubby post-pubescent body was squeezed into a lime green nylon uniform dress, causing it to wrinkle around her midriff. I thought she was exquisite. She told me she was 18. I lied about my own age. "Er, would you by any chance be around later?" I ventured, mentally postponing my departure from Chiclayo until the following day. Yes, she would ... great! ... though not until 11.00 p.m. She removed one of her earrings and presented it to me as a gift. I spent an unreasonable amount of time lingering over my *pollo y papas fritas*.

I chose a hotel close to the reataurant, though at a sufficiently discreet distance. I didn't want Milagro to think I was some kind of stalker. Any hopes of keeping a low profile were thwarted, however. The Chief of Police, a bunch of road workers and seemingly half the population of Chiclayo turned up to watch me negotiate my bike into the foyer of my hotel. The receptionist agreed to let me park it in the conference room for added security.

I met up with Milagro as arranged. The whole town was deserted at that time of night. We chatted and did a couple of laps of the Plaza de Armas. I retired to my hotel feeling like a dirty old man.

*   *   *   *

Leaving the bustle of Chiclayo in the morning rush-hour I got on the gas, leaving a wake of little yellow Daewoo 'Tiko' taxis, that swarmed like suicidal ants around the crumbling streets. It felt good to be free of their incessant honking.

The Panamericana unfurled into desert with an occasional semi-abandoned oasis. Packs of vultures hovered about me. I had heard that this desolate stretch of road was favoured by muggers. Several cyclists had been attacked and it was now regarded as a no-go zone for slow-moving traffic. Were the vultures awaiting my demise? Having the fastest vehicle in Peru offered me some consolation.

Passing through Sullana late morning I witnessed an impressive martial display. I was told by the very affable Captain (to whom I embarrassingly referred as Sergeant) that the *Dia de la Bandera* (flag day) is an event of great national pride in Peru. The Peruvians may well have an economy that lurches from one disaster to another, but they certainly know how to put on a show. The uniforms were dazzling in best Latin American fashion – buttons sparkled, boots were polished a patent sheen. How come they never win battles? They certainly look as though they should.

I chatted with the Captain, complimenting him on the appearance of his men. The inevitable crowd gathered round us: "Cuantos dollares?" "Que velocidad?" "De donde eres?": how much money ... what speed ... where are you from ... The questions came thick and fast. I've taught myself to stand there, patiently answering the probing questions of nosy locals. I have to remind myself that if the highlight of their day is the passing of the local bus or a knackered old truck/taxi donkey, then I represent something of a bonanza.

Forking off at Sullana in favour of the old, mainly disused, leg of the Panamericana, I stopped at a small town called Las Lomas. It reminded me of an elderly spinster I once knew called Miss Lomas. She lived alone and, like a lot elderly people, her kitchen was in total disarray. I always resisted her pressing offers to eat there.

I certainly didn't like the look of her namesake. An old woman and her daughter tried to convince me to eat in a squalid little café, clearly owned by one of their nearest and dearest. I instantly felt my throat constrict. "Muchas gracias señoras, pero voy a ir al Ecuador ahora," (I'd really love to eat with you, but must fly!) Trying desperately to extricate myself, I backed out. The old bird wasn't going to let me leave that easily, her daughter thrust her own two daughters forward – they were all of twelve years apiece. Did I like *negra* girls? "Not when they're 12!" I replied in horror. Grandma just cackled in the background, offering words of encouragement. I made a dash for the border.

The border offered little more in dining options. I had a couple of kebabs from a roadside brazier. The fried banana was good, but the meat of a very dubious origin. Had the mangy looking dogs scratching around my ankles been able to speak, I'm sure they'd be telling me one of their mates had gone missing.

At Customs, I delicately side-stepped the question of my non-existent *carnet de passages*. I had not bothered to get one, knowing that most South American officials neither knew nor cared what this bond document was. I produced some important-looking letters of introduction from the charity I was representing and, thankfully, the Ecuador Embassy in London. They seemed to satisfy the over-zealous official.

A police sergeant invited me into his office for no apparent reason – I could see a bribe on the horizon. I dropped into the role of visiting English policeman – it had worked before. "Ah, so you are secret agent, yes? How are you Mister James Bond? Perhaps you could leave a little tip for me – say $50?" This greatly amused the assembled throng. I didn't care. I was in Ecuador and it felt good.

Chapter 12

Trilby Hats and Police Brutality – Ecuador

I felt an instant culture change on riding into Ecuador. It felt poorer; it is, after all, the second poorest country in South America. The scenery was stunning – a rich carpet of emerald green smothered the hilly terrain. Condors hovered above and brightly plumed small birds soared across my path.

The bowler hat favoured by the Bolivians had been superseded by a rather jaunty trilby, favoured by men and women alike. The people seemed more at one with their environment. They appeared to respect their environment and delicate eco-system – something I had not noticed in Peru.

I enjoyed swinging the BM through Ecuador's rolling southern sierra, until I reached Loja, a promising-looking medium sized town that seemed friendly. I booked myself into a cavernous 60s-style suite of a rambling hotel. I had a private dining room where I could perhaps treat my guests to a fine vintage wine from Ecuador served in glasses that you would reject as a free gift with five litres of unleaded. Still, at £11 a night who's complaining?

I took an evening stroll through the unlit streets of Loja. It was not long before I was accosted by Alejandra, a 23-year-old girl promenading with her aunt and cousin. In a gesture of great largesse, I invited them to have dinner with me – not as magnanimous a gesture as it would at first seem as here you can feed a large family for the price of one person in Britain. It was a fine meal; *locro de papas* (potato and cheese soup) followed by the Ecuador version of *ceviche*, being more of a stew with a side order of popcorn immersed in the liquid, making it nice and soggy.

The following morning, Alejandra was waiting at the door of the hotel with two of her friends who wanted to meet me. A crowd started to gather around the bike along with a policeman who wanted to fine me for riding down a one-way street. Despite my guilt, I appealed to the crowd for support who gleefully took the opportunity to harangue the poor policeman. Police in much of Latin America have an image close to that of a pond-dwelling creature Any opportunity to have a go at the beleaguered individuals is greeted with relish.

Alejandra suggested that we go to her place for a photo session and a little more privacy.

She lived in a neat cubic development built around a small courtyard, populated by a few cats and chickens. As guest of honour, various ancient aunts were wheeled out to greet me. I was eager to get on the road, but they were not going to let me go that easily – chicken tamales and coffee were set before me. Each time I tried to politely draw the visit to a close, the girls had to "pop out for more camera batteries". Two hours and much beaming and posing later I bid them farewell.

I rode a mountain trail to Cuenca, the capital of the province. Tarmac soon gave way to dirt. Passing through a highland village I contemplated lunch, watched a group of villagers tearing strips off a fly-infested pig's corpse and decided to hang on till later.

Cuenca is a beautiful town – crammed with neatly formed churches in an appealing colonial centre. It's second only to Quito in its historical treasures. I was tempted to stay there but decided it was too early to call it a day. Big mistake! Soon villages dwindled away as I climbed still higher. A thick mist shrouded everything, not helped by the pitch darkness. I strained to make out livestock roaming in the road, which by now had dramatically declined to

An everyday Ecuadorean sight – truck crash near Cuenca

rubble. Heavy rain turned the road into a quagmire. I was back to standing on the pegs. Even the long suspension travel of the G.S. bottomed out on some of the cavernous potholes that pitted the road. I would occasionally make out a pinprick of light in the distance. Desperately hoping it was a village with warmth, dryness and food, my hopes would be dashed as I came across a cluster of dank little huts with trilby-hatted impassive broad faces staring out at me, without a flicker of emotion.

The half centimetre on the map had been hours. My underpants felt like a wet mulch. I limped into Chunchi with a dreary resignation to my shattered hopes. Anyone who is under the misapprehension that a night in an Ecuador hill village is a romantic and 'fun' thing to do, must not have been to Chunchi. I found a hotel – overpriced at £1 a night. With foreboding, I braced myself for an evening of beer and crackers – safe sustenance for my yearning hunger. *"No hay"* – the all-encompassing Spanish negative – was the answer to my request for beer at the first bar. It did have four Indians who stared at me unflinchingly while I disconsolately munched on dry crackers and sipped water. I attempted to outstare them but found them to be completely unaware of their rudeness. There and then, I made it a policy to try and find larger towns to stay in. Hill towns are interesting by day but deadly by night.

Escaping from my little cell at the crack of dawn, I reflected on how nights like the last one made the prospect of even the most mundane city a thrill-a-minute. Two hours later I was in Riobamba, a town where the great man himself, Simon Bolivar, once laid down his hat between battles. His house is something of a non-event but Riobamba is a pleasing medium-sized town. Having been denied edible food for 24 hours I practically threw myself prostrate on the doorstep of the Café Monte Carlo, a much-favoured place with gringo backpackers – and rightly so. The owner goes to great pains to explain from where his food is sourced, and the purity of his water thanks to an expensive filtration system. I met a pretty Welsh girl over some truly gratifying scrambled eggs. Susan was doing some holiday backpacking and was heading for Quito, like me. We made plans to meet up there in a few days. Her lovely South Wales lilt was intoxicating – words fell from her lips like silver dollars.

While she, the café owner and myself were chatting on the sidewalk outside, a small film crew spotted the bike. They were hotfooting it to a job but wanted to interview me on the spot for a local news channel. A very pushy woman was thrusting her clearly embarrassed teenage daughter forward and exclaiming to the clearly uninterested journalists (or anyone else who may have been interested) "Look! She is a journalist too!" I felt sorry for the poor girl.

*   *   *   *

I stopped at a small village on the way to Quito where a horse market was taking place. Parking up beside the corral, I casually sauntered up to a group of Indians while trying to avoid drawing attention to myself. No chance of that – a hundred pairs of eyes locked onto me like Exocet missiles. I was hoping for some surreptitious shots of Indian horse traders at work, using my Sigma 80-300 zoom lens. As they gathered around and peered at my and my bike I decided to seek out the 'leader' – there's always one, usually the one with the fairest skin. There's little point in asking an indigenous person if you can take their photo – it's either met with a point-blank refusal or occasionally a demand for a 'posing fee'. But find the leader and paint a wonderful vista about how it's going to make him a famous and desirable celebrity by appearing in my book and/or the Wilmslow Express Advertiser, and vanity will soon get the better of him. Soon his flock will be grinning broadly and posing whichever way you like.

I swept past the resort town of Baño, known not unsurprisingly for its thermal baths and saw Tungurahua, the famous active volcano smoking gently in the distance. As I approached the outskirts of Quito there was a torrential downpour, turning the diesel-soaked dirt road into a skating ring. I watched a car brake hard, lock up and pile into the back of a truck. I left my brakes well alone and used engine braking to decelerate. Despite an ominous approach past dreary factories, car bodyshops and sundry industrial and commercial heaps of detritus, Quito proved a pleasant surprise. Nestling in a hollow at the foot of the volcano Pichincha, it is effectively in two parts – an old colonial city and a new financial centre housing banks and hotels, which is where I would stay. Luxury is what I needed after the previous night's deprivations, so I checked into the very opulent Colon Hilton.

Unwinding in the hotel's gym, I was engaged in conversation

with a lady whom I first thought was Thai, but was in fact Peruvian – the difference in appearance can be negligible. Ruth is multilingual and very well travelled, she runs the Latin American operation of a world-wide human rights organisation. Her 'speciality' is the murky world of police brutality, a role her previous job as Peru's first and only police captain had equipped her for admirably.

One thing led to another and we wound up having dinner in a very luxurious Thai restaurant. I was beginning to realise that what Ruth wants, she gets. She had berated the taxi driver on the way there for the standard of his driving (which by Ecuador standards seemed OK to me), followed by the hapless waiter who'd had the temerity to keep her waiting two-and-a-half minutes. I sensed that my turn would be next. I had been holding my knife and fork correctly (years of drilling from my father) but was feeling the gaze of Ruth's critical eye. She reeled off a long list of her expectations of males and gave a resumé of her recent boyfriends, particularly a Norwegian banker, who was described as 'unsatisfactory'. I realised that having reached the pinnacle of her career, Ruth's next 'project' was to find a husband and she was approaching the matter with an attention to detail to be expected from a high-ranking police officer. I felt as if I was a client of a computer dating agency at interview.

I met Ruth for breakfast in the hotel and wished I hadn't. Over scrambled eggs she proceeded to tell me in detail of the operations she had had on her ovarian cyst, sparing no expense in the gore department.

*   *   *   *

Quito is crammed with small language schools teaching Spanish to travellers. Along with Antigua, Guatemala, it is one of the cheapest and best places to study Spanish in the Americas, which is why I found myself being grilled on reflexive verbs that afternoon by Irene in a cubby hole of an office purporting to be a 'language academy'. I had taken a three-hour lesson, the majority of which we used to discuss the malaise of the Ecuador economy. (Ecuador's economic problems extend well beyond a three-hour discussion). She cited a change in government along with some high-level corruption as the principal cause of a fall in the value of the

Campesinos, Guatemala

sucre from 6,000 sucres to the dollar in 1999 to 25,000 sucres to the dollar in 2000. With an ever-increasing national debt the country was in dire straits. A national average salary of US $700 p.a. along with an average house cost of $20,000 spells a grim future for Ecuadoreans. This is beginning to reveal itself in the high incidence of crime, urban suicide and marital conflict.

I took Irene for a meal to a nearby Tex-Mex restaurant. It was nothing special but had she paid it would have taken care of about three days' earnings. She told me about her hobbies, of which she had many: making jewellery, writing poetry and traditional Ecuadorean music to name but a few. It was cheering to hear of someone leading a normal life in the midst of such economic hardship. Some months later I received a letter from Irene pleading with me to lend her the airfare to Spain. The situation in Ecuador has become intolerable and she was trying to get out.

I had hoped to make an early start the following day and maybe make it to Popayan in Colombia. I squandered my time advantage on bike and kit cleaning duties. I resigned myself to the prospect of leaving my five-star luxo-haven for the dubious attraction of

Colombian immigration. The phone rang. It was Susan from South Wales. I invited her to the Hilton for a late breakfast and my departure was shelved for 24 hours.

I've always felt that when touring, if you get up in the morning and really don't want to swing your leg over the saddle then you should award yourself a day off (schedule allowing) and enjoy the local attractions. Susan was not local but she was very attractive. Unfortunately, Ruth breezed into the dining room after us. She gave me a look of pity that implied I knew no better, being a weak and impressionable man. She gave Susan her most withering glare. Fortunately, Susan was engrossed in her fruit salad by this time, oblivious to the disdain being directed towards her. We made plans to visit the market town of Otobalo.

Five hours each way, grinding up mountainsides on an overcrowded ancient bus, just to view a few handmade shawls may seem a pointless exercise ... it certainly did to me, but Susan, a veteran of the gringo trail, had spent many hours on Latin American buses and took it in her stride. She later admitted that the market had been 'touristy' but I knew the alternative. The locals' market usually offers little more than the opportunity to acquire a fifth-hand electric fire or a few dried llama foetuses. I pondered this fact on the bus back to Quito while an overweight Indian lady used my knee as a stool. We went for a typical Ecuadorean dinner that night: *humitas*, tender ground corn steamed in corn leaves, washed down with *marocho*, a mix of *mate*, cinnamon, milk and sugar served hot. We did a couple of bars – karaoke and Cuban. We danced the bomba. I collapsed into bed – drunk, danced-out and exhausted.

Knowing I could not lose another day, I dragged myself out of my luxurious king-sized bed and packed my kit up for a lunchtime start. I could have happily passed more time in Quito, but my morbid fascination for that most dangerous of Latin American countries – Colombia – was driving me on. The sea journey from Colombia to Panama was becoming something of an unknown quantity too. Despite my exhaustive research, even to the extent of trawling through reports in the library of the Royal Geographical Society, nobody could tell me definitely if it could be done with a motorcycle. I had a rough idea of how long it would take to get through each country (usually wildly inaccurate) but the search for a boat ... impossible to say.

Beauty abounded in the fertile and semi-tropical lands north of Quito. A most unusual sight greeted me in a village outside Ibarra. I had got used to seeing a greater concentration of indigenous Indians at high altitude throughout South America, but here was a low-lying tropical village populated exclusively with people of African descent. Having not seen more than a handful of black people since Tierra del Fuego, it came as something of a surprise. Knowing how, with the passing of the centuries, black people have adapted to cold climates, i.e. to cities like Detroit, I was bemused by their need to congregate in this remote village with no visible economic means of support, solely for its climate.

Chapter 13

Danger in Paradise – Welcome to Colombia

I finally arrived at the Colombian border at Ipiales. Like most gringos who have been spoon-fed negative media images of Colombian violence, I fully expected a line of machine-gun toting paramilitaries at the border – eyes narrowed menacingly behind their Ray-Bans. What I actually found was a pleasant, softly-spoken immigration official working out of a modern air-conditioned office. He explained that, being Sunday, the office that issues temporary vehicle import licences had closed early. I was stamped in but the bike was not, forcing me to spend the night in Ipiales in order to retrieve it from the appropriate officials in the morning.

Ipiales is a nondescript small town, though with a greater level of prosperity than its neighbouring towns in Ecuador. I found a nice, clean little hotel for $19. Watching TV in a restaurant that evening, the coverage was almost exclusively cycling or football. I had heard of the national obsession with both sports, though my only real insight into the importance of football was when a player from the national squad had the misfortune to be executed for conceding an important goal after the last World Cup. I decided to keep my love of Manchester United to myself.

Strolling the streets of Ipiales that night, I watched little boys chasing each other on their bicycles, little girls proudly parading their white-frilled Sunday best, and old men playing cards in tiny plazas while their plump, floral printed wives chatted on street corners. It was hard to imagine, witnessing these scenes of normality, how bloody Colombia's past had been.

After liberating Colombia from the Spanish along with what are now Ecuador and Venezuela, Simon Bolivar told the revolutionary Congress of his success, who in turn proclaimed the region as Gran Colombia. This was as recently as 1819. A general Congress was held at Cucuta in 1821 where divisions soon became apparent between those seeking centralisation and others who desired a federation of sovereign states. Bolivar, favouring centralisation, got his way, but it was not to last long. Venezuela went its own way in 1829 followed by Ecuador in 1830. After a brief period under the name Nueva Granada, the name Colombia was resurrected in 1863. The centralists and federalists, who went under the banners of Conservative and Liberal respectively, continued their early disagreements. Various civil wars ensued culminating in a Liberal revolt in 1899 that soon became the 'War of the Thousand Days'. It only lasted for three years, but by the time the Liberals were defeated 100,000 people had been killed.

Violence raised its ugly head again in 1948 after a period of relative peace between the two parties. Of nine years' duration, 'La Violencia' as it was known, resulted in the deaths of 300,000 people, a staggering figure, even by Colombia's bloody standards. A truce of sorts was agreed, whereby both parties supported the same presidential candidate and divided control equally. This was effectively ended in 1978, though some agreements continued until 1986.

The word guerilla is practically synonymous with Colombia. Guerilla groups proliferated during this period. There were four major players, the most well-known outside Colombia being FARC (Fuerzas Armadas Revolucionarias de Colombia) the left-wing guerilla group. FARC, like the IRA, has a political arm and won seats in Congress. In a bid to secure peace, the Government has handed large areas of the country to them, which in effect they control.

Throughout the 1980s Colombia's two main narcotics cartels, the Medellin and Cali, put Colombia on the international map. Pablo Escobar, or El Padre as he was known to the beneficiaries of his largesse, needs no introduction. Listed by Forbes magazine as the world's seventh wealthiest man, he launched a long assault without precedent on those that got in the way of his ruthless ambitions. His campaign of bombings, kidnappings and executions left the country reeling. His most outrageous attack came when he sent a courier onto a commercial Avianca airliner. The courier was unaware of the true contents of his carry-on case. But the bomb he had been carrying detonated killing all 110 passengers. Ironically,

President Gaviria, the target for the bomb had decided some weeks earlier not to take the flight.

In 1991 Escobar was eventually imprisoned in La Catedral situated outside Medellin. The prison was the ultimate in luxury. Here he and his cronies smoked dope, brought in young prostitutes and generally continued the high-life, while the guards, being in Escobar's pocket, turned a blind eye – even when ostentatious furnishings, bathroom suites and telecommunications equipment were brought in.

From here he calmly continued to run his empire. Escobar had always been expert at massaging public opinion through clever use of PR and developing an image of 'friend of the poor', but by now Colombians were growing weary of the endless shootings, bombings and kidnappings. Soon a vigilante group (nobody quite knew who was behind them) called Los Pepes began a reign of terror, executing some of Escobar's 'sicarios' (hit-men) and fringe members of his family. Escobar went on the run and after millions of dollars had been spent tracking him down he was eventually gunned down by a joint Colombian/American search bloc.

Throughout all this time Colombia had been besieged, not only by the *narcotraficos*, but by left-wing guerilla groups, right-wing paramilitaries and 'death squads', along with straightforward contract killings and kidnappings. It became impossible to deduce who had planted the last bomb. The list of likely candidates was endless.

It was with this comforting thought that I set off the following lunchtime – I had wasted the morning which I had spent in the DAS (Departamento Adminastrativo de Seguridad de Colombia) office, watching three people trying to type one form on an antiquated typewriter.

*   *   *   *

I did not have to get far out of Ipiales to be plunged into the most gorgeous scenery of cascading waterfalls, breathtaking gorges and lush tropical vegetation, each tree bearing some kind of exotic fruit or other – guayaba, maracuya, curuba, guanabana and more. There were plenty of bananas too, though nowhere near the quantity found in Ecuador. Ecuadoreans feed their swine on bananas, being the cheapest and most available foodstuff. I remembered an Ecuadorean restaurateur telling me with an incredulous look: "I have been told that in Israel people have actually been offered a banana as a desert" as though this was the ultimate insult that could befall a human being.

Motorcycles are very popular in Colombia, though rarely is a bike over 500cc seen, the majority being low-capacity Enduro machines. It's illegal for two males to ride together. I at first assumed that this was some bizarre law to combat homosexuality but it is quite obviously to prevent drive-by shootings. Colombian 'sicarios', or contract killers, favour this means of transport. I did see a Honda Cub 90 being ridden by a man and pillioned by his wife, young daughter and dog. I was tempted to ask if the dog was female!

I attempted a photograph some schoolgirls. I thought they made a nice shot in their bright red smocks and crisp white blouses with a great backdrop of emerald green mountains. As they crossed the road to walk on the other side, eyeing me with suspicion, I felt acutely embarrassed. I could see them saying "Say, Maria de Jesús, see that gringo over there? Is he weird or what!"

I stopped at a lowland village for a 'Hit'. No, that's not an inhalation of cocaine, but a proprietary brand of Colombian carbonated lemon juice. The locals, all of whom were black, were engaged in the amusing spectacle of chasing a runaway hog down the main road. Little boys were leaping around waving their arms around to little effect while the hog ducked and dived like Jeffrey Archer.

Between Pesto and Popayan, I began to notice a disturbing frequency of FARC graffiti. I had read that this road was known as a hot-spot for guerilla activity. I was beginning to feel a little uneasy. Both sides of the road were densely foliated, providing perfect cover for an ambush. It's easy to be lulled into a false sense of security in such a stunning country inhabited, in the main, by friendly outgoing people. If I ever needed a wake-up call I only needed to switch on the TV news to see images of bullet-riddled cars and interviews with sobbing widows.

The only net benefit of all this human suffering is that tourists are scared witless to visit Colombia, enabling me to find a luxurious room in a converted monastery for the modest sum of $36, Popayan's finest accommodation.

I had just ridden into town, admiring the endless streets of Andalucian-style colonial architecture, when a lady called Marisol approached me to warn me of the dangers that lurked within the Popayan. We chatted on the sidewalk at length and I decided that she was not in the narcotics-terrorism game, so gratefully accepted her offer to meet later for a 'tour'.

We met in my hotel's reception later that evening and I was treated to a whistle-stop tour of the city by somebody who clearly knew her local history. She showed me the Cathedral and the beautiful Iglesia de Santo Domingo, the former having been rebuilt after practically being destroyed by an earthquake in 1983. Founded in 1537, the town soon became popular with wealthy Spanish families who owned sugar haciendas in the Cali region. It has retained all its colonial charm and shows very little impact from the 20th century.

Marisol and I had dinner in a restaurant in the *barrio* where she lived. It might seem that all I do is take women out to dinner, but apart from anything else, it's important to have trustworthy allies in a country like this, and women are easier to trust. The restaurant was typically Antioquian with traditional paraphernalia: straw hats, ornate saddles and horse brasses hanging from the ceiling. The Colombians are keen horsemen – none more so than in Antioquia – the department of which Medellin is the capital. We ate *churrasco* and *Bandeja Paisa* respectively, the latter being an Antioquian speciality of minced beef, *frijoles* (beans), *chorizo* (spicy sausage), rice, *patacon* (fried plantain), a fried egg, *chicharron* (fried pork rind), *arepa* (a toasted maize pancake) and finally avocado. It's not a dish to be taken immediately before going to bed.

I enjoyed a restful morning, soaking up the atmosphere of this engaging town before meeting Marisol and her young son, Jose Fernandez, for lunch. I had not expected to eat lunch in what amounted to someone's front room out in the barrio. The idea of paying the owner of the house after eating felt a little odd. We visited a friend of Marisol's who operated a hairdressing salon in her front room (actually, it was her garage). It seemed to me that Popayan had a thriving cottage industry – which is one way to avoid paying protection money to guerilla groups.

Marisol lives in a pleasant barrio of low-level bungalows. She and her son enjoy a decent standard of living, though not what you would expect for someone with a doctorate and a seat at the local university.

After a frustrating search for a *casa de cambios* to change money the following morning – further evidence, if it were needed, of the lack of overseas visitors to Popayan – I hit the road for Medellin. I only got a few kilometres out of Popayan when I picked up a slow puncture in my back tyre. Luckily it happened within yards of a tyre repairer's shack. Ten minutes later the offending nail had been removed, tyre re-sealed and I was on my way having parted with the princely sum of $1. I felt pleased with myself and generally at peace with the world. That was to be short-lived.

Chapter 14

Kidnap Capital of the World

I stopped for lunch outside Buga at what seemed like a pleasant palm-fronded affair. There was hardly anybody eating and I noticed a distinctly uneasy atmosphere. While waiting for my food, I wandered into the adjoining bar – big mistake! It was crowded with wealthy-looking men – no women. They all turned round in unison and stared hard at me, like an unwanted guest. Each and every one of them had a handgun stuffed down his waistband. I backed out, trying to smile politely and play the dumb foreign tourist. As I ripped away from the dirt parking lot, spewing red earth from my back tyre, I glanced at the vehicles lined up: Porsches, Mercedes, gleaming Chevy trucks with blacked-out windows. They hinted at earnings not made from selling mangoes. My first brush with the drug czars did not fill me with optimism about my next stop, Medellin, home of the world's most violent cocaine cartel.

I rapidly gained altitude as I neared Medellin, through mountains of remarkable verdancy and endless tiers of coffee plantations. Colombia is reputed to be the producer of the world's finest quality coffees. Unfortunately, the choicest beans are exported, leaving the dregs for local consumption. Most cups of coffee I've had in Colombia have ranged from dire to merely palatable. This region lying immediately south of Medellin goes by the somewhat predictable name of the Zona Cafetera. The coffee plantations are to be found at about 1500 metres where they're tended diligently by straw-hatted *campesinos*. I was riding through in mid-May at the peak of the rainy season and was about to experience the worst of it. The first drops fell in big globules – it felt as though someone had spat at me. Minutes later I was in a deluge. I had to find cover on this already treacherous mountain trail. I scrabbled frantically to get my waterproofs on, only succeeding in trapping more water inside than out. Lightning forked dramatically, momentarily illuminating the gunmetal sky. I decided to take refuge in what looked like a roadside bar. As I walked into the gloomy hut I was confronted with my greatest fear; two dozen combat-uniformed men, all clutching machine guns or automatic rifles. "Oh, dear God – it's FARC" was my first thought, their uniforms barely differing from those of the regular army. It was only a small mercy that they proved to be regular soldiers – their activities often merge, in this ultra-sensitive region, where soldiers of any denomination are regarded with mistrust. I tried to lighten the tangibly threatening atmosphere by encouraging them to have photos taken with the bike and emphasising the humanitarian angle of my trip, leading the conversation into safe areas. It worked! They gradually turned their attentions to mercilessly teasing the 15-year-old bar owner's daughter, taunting the poor child with crude sexual suggestions. As the downpour eased off, I headed off after their chilling words of advice to be vigilant for guerilla activity.

The climb to Medellin was a nightmare: a steep, treacherous, filthy road punctuated by hairpin bends. It was pitch black with no street lamps and teeming rain. I was caught in a long caravan of soot-belching trucks with little or no chance of overtaking them, such was the visibility. A further two hours of riding around Medellin getting progressively more lost did nothing to improve my mood. It was very late, I needed a good hotel – somewhere I could clean and dry my filthy gear.

Wet, dirty and tired, I staggered into the luxurious lobby of the Hotel Dann Carlton. I would not have been surprised had the receptionist politely directed me to the nearest refuge for homeless people, but to his credit, he knocked the price down from $100 a night to a very reasonable $65, once he had learned of my mission. I often found in my time in Latin America that five-star hotels offer good value for money – as long as you stay away from the mini-bar.

Stephanie, a 17-year-old Californian girl, had been lolling around at reception. She wanted to hear my story so we had a drink in the bar. *Tres Esquinas* rum on the rocks never tasted so good as it did after a day like that. Stephanie, I discovered, had Colombian parents but had been raised in the USA, explaining her MTV-speak. I at first dismissed her as a precocious and rather spoilt brat but gradually warmed to her as I learnt about her fascinating background. Her father, at the time a low-ranking police officer near Medellin, discovered a disused emerald mine and staked his claim. It proved to be a source of abundant emeralds which he and his wife now trade in internationally. It did not prove hard to figure out that, with two practically permanent rooms at the Dann Carlton, they were doing rather well at it.

Medellin is a thrusting go-ahead city, full of enterprising, hard-working people trying to shrug off the city's violent past. With the possible exception of the night I arrived, it enjoys a good climate. Downtown skyscrapers and glass edifices gleamed prosperously in the morning sunshine. I decided it was a place in which I might like to live.

                    *   *   *   *

The road north from Medellin, through Antioquia, is endlessly twisting, encouraging spirited riding. This was marred by another endless stream of trucks heading for the coastal ports. Judging by the amount of goods vehicles flooding in and out of the city it was not hard to understand its reputation as the industrial heartland of Colombia. Climbing one mountain, I came across a long tailback of stationary trucks stretching for about two kilometres. Fearing the worst – a guerilla roadblock – I was relieved to see the road had been cordoned for the Colombian national cycle race – a kind of Tour de Colombia. This was to cause me a one-and-a-half hour delay, but it gave me an opportunity to make a new friend. Phillipe, a young student, was heading off to a remote farmhouse in Cordoba with two friends for a couple of days. He spoke excellent English gained from racing go-karts in Indianapolis, Indiana. Sadly, Colombian companies don't have a pile of spare cash available to sponsor such rising national stars, so his dreams had to be put on hold. I met up with them at various re-fuelling and food pit-stops as we made our way north. They shared their lunch with me and invited me to the farm, but I had to press on.

It soon became clear that I was not going to make Cartagena by nightfall so I stopped at a *criolla* barbecue pit in Caucasia, a sleepy little town on the banks of the River Cauca, to assess the situation. Riding through the badlands after nightfall would be tantamount to suicide so I took the advice of Adriana, the beautiful young waitress, and checked in to the Meson del Gitano, the bedroom balconies of which opened out onto dense rain forest, alive with the screeching of exotic birds.

The heat and humidity were intense here. My legs, encased in leather, were running with perspiration before I had even left my room. I would make it a policy to always wear my armoured Dainese Gore-Tex jacket on any road other than a deserted dead-straight desert one. I wasn't looking forward to donning it today. Over breakfast, a man with a flowing silver mane of hair, belying his youthful features, told me conspiratorially "Don't deviate from the Panamericana. The road that runs parallel to it (the one I had planned to use) is crawling with guerillas, almost as far as Cartagena". A second, separate young man, who was clearly well-travelled and intelligent enough to know the difference between real and perceived danger, backed this up. He told me he never used the roads in Colombia, in fact *nobody* with any sense used them. Those who were able to flew from town to town. He went on to tell me in lurid detail about FARC sympathisers who worked in banks and would surreptitiously feed information to the guerillas about the financial status of potential kidnap targets. Upwards of $1 million was the usual demand. I doubted that my banking adviser at the Royal Bank of Scotland in Wilmslow was 'in bed' with FARC, but my father's parting words rang in my ears as I headed for Cartagena: "Son, if there's a ransom involved – remember, you're on your own!" As he is a financially prudent Yorkshireman, I had taken him at his word.

Every few kilometres I would pass through roadblocks, either police or military. Another long line of trucks prompted me to fear the worst again, but this time it was a blockage caused by a crane dragging a jack-knifed lorry out of a ditch. Further up the road was something which haunted me for a long time: two dead horses at the edge of the road, one of which had been set on fire. Locals cycling past barely glanced at them.

*   *   *   *

It was with some relief that I joined the maelstrom of ancient buses, beat-up yellow taxis and kamikaze scooterists, funnelling into Cartagena, my last port of call in South America.

The coastal Colombians, or *costeños* as they're known, enjoy greater racial diversity than inhabitants of the interior. They have a distinctly Caribbean attitude to life and work which probably explains why it took two of them three times longer than it normally takes one person to wash my bike. Colombian timekeeping isn't exactly world-leading but the *costeños* take it to a new dimension. I resolved to learn the art of patience, though it did not fill me with great optimism about the search for a boat.

I checked into the Hotel Caribe in Bocagrande, Bocagrande being the heart of Cartagena's tourist zone. It is a stretch of mainly beach-front hotels, most of which are geared to package tourism. The beach is a no-no unless you enjoy being cajoled into buying cheap sunglasses and T-shirts at two-minute intervals. Of much greater interest is the historic centre of the town. Surrounded by ramparts – or *murallas* – punctuated by the occasional cannon, the historic centre is a living museum of churches and plazas. Founded by the Spanish in 1533 it became a staging post where the Spanish accumulated their plundered treasures from the Americas before shipping them back to Spain. Various nations, not least the English, attempted to relieve Cartagena of its treasures. In 1741 Sir Edward Vernon arrived with 27,000 men and 3,000 pieces of artillery and laid siege for 56 days. He was eventually thwarted by the one-armed, one-legged, one-eyed General Blas de Lezo (with a bit of help). Not England's finest hour I feel.

Deciding on an evening stroll, I stopped by at a small restaurant in Bocagrande and sat on the patio which opened out onto a busy street. There was a group of three other people eating at the far side of the patio and nobody else.

A skinny, wild-eyed black youth dressed in rags walked up to me. I assumed he wanted to sell me drugs or sunglasses, or maybe both. Backed into a corner, I soon realised that was not what he wanted as he produced an eight-inch pointed shard of glass from under his ragged shirt. His back blocked the view of the other diners who were oblivious as to what was going on. "I don't want a problem – just give me your money" he hissed. I had seconds to assess the situation. He looked high – probably glue, yet he was clearly in a nervous state, eyes darting from side to side. Despite the threat to my life, I felt strangely calm. "If you're hungry, take the meat". I gestured to it with my eyes. I just needed to buy some time to think. I only had about $30 on me, certainly not worth risking my life for, yet I was convinced he was too scared to carry out his threat. I stood my ground. It worked. He rolled his eyes, stuffed the pork chop into his mouth (it wasn't the greatest anyway) and

scarpered. The people at the far side of the patio had by now realised what had gone on. They offered profuse apologies and hoped it
had not given me a bad impression of their country, and very
kindly bought me a beer.

The following day I applied myself to the task of finding a
passage to Panama, the bike being by far the more difficult cargo to
place. Following my best lead to date, I went in search of the Swiss
owner of a small backpackers' hostel on Calle Media Luna, who
was believed to own two boats and to offer this service. I found the
'Chalet Suiza' deep in the heart of Cartagena's red-light district.
Getsemani, a poor barrio in the outer walled town, is not a place to
linger at night. I lost count of the times I was asked: "Hey, gringo!
you want fucky-fucky?"

The overweight, unshaven Swiss man hunched over the Chalet
Suiza's makeshift reception looked like a man who'd seen too
much of life. Too much partying and now the party was over. He
wearily explained that Cartagena had seen its best days. What tourism had existed had been frightened off by stories of violence and
narco-trafficking. Regrettably, he had sold both his boats and was
eking out a living from the odd backpacker. He was unable to
suggest an alternative, other than asking around at Club Nautico on
Manga Island, Cartagena's yacht club.

Club Nautico looked to be an inspiring place to start my search.
Yachts were lined up alongside two jetties. White hulls dazzled in
the tropical sun. I spoke to Guillermo who supervised the routine
operations of the nautical side of the club. He could not help me but
promised to keep his ear to the ground. Further asking around led
me to Dominic, a slight Belgian with the most piercing blue eyes I
had ever seen. He was multilingual, worldly-wise (he'd been travelling the seven seas on his one-man yacht for years), and with his
flowing blonde hair and high cheekbones he looked like a Viking
god. At least, he did until he opened his mouth. He appeared to
perform his own dentistry, no doubt with the help of the boat's
toolkit.

He offered to carry my bike for $700, a hefty sum, explaining it
would have to be stripped down to its smallest components, each
part to be sealed in polythene and located in different parts of the
boat for ballast. He spoke of removing electrics, forks, dropping the
engine from the frame, removing the drive shaft – the lot. As an

ex-diesel mechanic, he offered to assist me. I ran the likely scenario through my mind.

Firstly, I know salt water can ruin electrics and any type of polished surface and Dominic's diminutive vessel looked as though it would be pitched around like a piece of driftwood. Secondly, did I want to be pitched around like driftwood for a week, heaving my guts into the Atlantic at regular intervals? Thirdly, in the unlikely event that we got to Panama without losing most of the bike's components, who exactly would be standing on the dockside in the blazing heat for two days trying to re-assemble it? Dominic? I doubted it. It was payment up-front. My mechanical knowledge is fairly elementary. Even if parts had not been lost overboard or stolen from Panama's notoriously unsafe dockside, I know I would not be up to the re-assembly job. At this stage, Dominic had not even seen my bike. Once he saw it that afternoon, he agreed with me, it was too big a machine and too complex a task to perform.

I had missed the departure of a much larger boat which could have carried the bike complete. No further boats were due to depart for the next few weeks. It didn't look good. I was advised to contact 'Manfred', an Austrian shipping agent who invariably called into Club Nautico with the sole aim of drinking himself to oblivion. If I could catch Manfred when he was sober (apparently unusual) he may be able to find a freighter to carry me. You may be thinking: why not stick it on a pallet and fly it over? I had been advised by the Dutch round-the-world bikers that I had met in Bolivia that clearing their bikes through Customs in Panama had been the most frustrating experience of their three year trip, involving spending a whole week in a Customs shed trying to unravel a mass of bureaucratic tape. I did not like the idea of being separated from the bike.

I spent the whole of the following day lounging around at Club Nautico, the net result being lots of new friends, an increased knowledge of sailboats and Caribbean sailing routes and times, but little else. We sat around, my new buddies and I, chatting and drinking beer: Herman, a South African surfer who'd more or less shadowed my route from Tierra del Fuego, though on long-distance buses; Bob, a Californian who'd taken early retirement from Silicon Valley to sail the seas, and Irving and Judy (and their dog) doing the same. We exhausted every subject from the world order to boat maintenance, before adjourning to a nice little Arabic café for a dinner of falafel and kebabs.

I called Manfred the following morning, who told me in halting Teutonic English that he may have some promising news. He knew of an old rusting Haitian freighter (not the way he described it, but would a Haitian freighter be anything but?) departing tomorrow for Coco Solo, a port near Colon. He believed it was carrying bananas or coconuts. I knew if we could agree a price and complete the documentation in time it would be the perfect solution. Perfect – but very grim.

On the Sunday it rained all day – a veritable monsoon. I holed up in the Hotel Caribe all day, contemplating my options. I could not wait till Monday so I could get things rolling. Never has a Sunday felt so long. A Rotaract event was taking place by the hotel pool. A gang of stylish and attractive twenty-somethings strumming guitars, laughing and, no doubt, planning to sleep with each other afterwards was in stark contrast to a Rotaract gathering I once gate-crashed in south Cheshire where a dispirited cast of worthies was huddled over halves of shandy in a dismal pub function room planning their next hike in the rain.

As the rain eased, I took my camera into the historic centre for some atmospheric dusk shots. Camouflaged soldiers were the sole inhabitants; they were standing guard at government buildings, the stucco façades of which – lemon, blue, and terracotta – were peeling and decayed. Along with the humid night air it gave me the true flavour of this most exotic of ports.

Back at the hotel, Herman called me to tell me of his intention to come with me on the boat to Panama. This would be good, not only for the company, but to have another pair of watchful eyes on my belongings. Things improved further when I turned up at the Club Nautico. Maye, the lovely, dusky girl who often worked at the bar, was taking a night off. Would she like to join me for dinner down-town? Yes, she would. We ate (I ate, she watched) in the Plaza Santo Domingo, in what would have been a very romantic setting had we not been besieged by hordes of street vendors, offering all manner of performances, services and goods. Fire eaters, picture sellers, rose vendors, troubadours, cigarette girls and even some bloke who would put electric shocks through your arms by inviting you to pass a metal ring over an electrified wire. I failed to see the 'unique selling point' of this service.

Maye was in her final year at university studying psychology. She's exotic looking with mainly Spanish and Indian blood, along with traces of Italian and African. She particularly endeared herself to me when she guessed my age to be "just a little more" than hers. Sixteen years more to be precise.

*   *   *   *

I called at Manfred's apartment early the following morning. A florid-faced Austrian with bright ginger hair and a broad matching moustache answered the door. The thing that most struck me was his huge pot-belly incongruously hanging above his normally proportioned pink legs. He was wearing a white T-shirt, stained from the previous night's dinner and grubby blue shorts. He surveyed me through bloodshot weary eyes and beckoned me in with a grunt. He padded over to the kitchen, his bare pink soles slopping heavily on the tiles, to prepare a coffee. Viewing the fallout of the previous night's activities – overflowing ashtrays, crumpled beer cans, empty bottles of rum and, not least, Manfred's belly straining against his T-shirt, I decided that this was a man who liked a drink. Shortly after, Herman turned up with two fresh-faced English undergraduates who had tracked him down at the Club Nautico. Matt and Adrian desperately wanted to take a boat to Panama, their 'isn't-this-a-great-adventure?' youthful enthusiasm was soon dampened by Manfred's gruff, world-weary directness: "You boys will take ze plane to Panama City – I vill give you seaman's papers and you vill pretend to be seamen". The boys nodded eagerly at the prospect of a discounted seaman's ticket. Herman had no such luck. Being South African he would need a visa, and a few calls to the relevant authorities told us that he would miss both the boat and the plane due to its delay. I resigned myself to the fact that I was on my own – no company and nobody to share the cost.

I discovered that the freighter had been delayed by a day. It had suffered damage after a collision with a pier. This did not worry me. What did, was that the damage was being paid for out of the crew's wages who by now had not been paid for eight weeks. At best, I predicted a heightened interest in my valuables; at worst, a mutiny.

That afternoon I rode down to Club Nautico to say my farewells to Herman, whom I had grown to like over the few days. I squeezed Maye onto my single seat and took her over to Bocagrande for a night out. Navigating the Cartagena traffic with a shared seat and one set of footpegs was not easy.

Determined to regain my mental equilibrium, I spent the following morning relaxing by the pool before checking out and riding over to Manfred's where I was to drop off my belongings for storage until sailing time. At this point things started to go wrong.

The skipper of the Haitian coastal freighter stated that on no account was he to carry a passenger or extra cargo. We managed to locate another vessel – this time a freighter with a San Andrean crew. San Andres is the principal island in an archipelago located off the east coast of Nicaragua but owned by Colombia. Natives of the island speak a type of Jamaican-English along with Spanish, a legacy of the previous British colonisation of 1631. Pirates continued to use the main islands of San Andres and Providencia as a base where they would lie in wait for Spanish galleons loaded with treasures and bound for the Old World.

After achieving independence from Britain, Colombia claimed the sovereignty of the islands, fiercely disputed by the Government of Nicaragua. The native inhabitants, who are descended from Jamaican slaves, try to retain the English-Caribbean culture, though this is fast becoming diluted by the hordes of Colombian duty-free shoppers who invade the island each year.

I spoke to Captain Felix Newbold, skipper of the *Clara E* to negotiate my passage. He stood firm at $600 and wouldn't even drop $50. He knew there were no alternatives and had me over a barrel. Manfred and I drove over to Pasa Caballo, a decrepit little port forty minutes out of town. We drove down dirt trails past ramshackle huts overflowing with poor black families. Semi-naked children played in the piles of detritus lining the streets. Scrawny chickens flapped their wings at our approach. The sun was beating down unmercifully. My worst fears were confirmed when we escaped the maze of dirt roads and eventually came across the *Clara E* sitting forlornly alongside two other rusting hulks. Boarding the *Clara E*, a grizzled islander in a grubby beige nylon safari suit and a sailor's cap approached us. He looked at us with amusement then enquired "I suppose you boys would be Eu-ro-pee-ans," in his thick island patois. "Welcome aboard the *Clara E*". Captain Felix showed me around the vessel, not a long job, considering the galley and mess room, traditionally among the larger rooms on a boat, were only about four square metres. Descending through a trapdoor into the bowels of the boat, I was practically overcome by the suffocating humidity and heat, the reek of oil and the clatter that came from the old Perkins diesel. I shuddered at the sight of my cabin. An indescribably filthy mattress and a pile of discarded engine parts was its centrepiece. Damp clung to the rusty bulkhead. I suspected the cabin had not been cleaned since its maiden voyage in the late 1950s. Manfred suspected that Captain Felix's claims that we would set sail that night were optimistic. He told me the skipper had some outstanding port dues to pay and would be going nowhere until they were settled. So we adjourned to Club Nautico to await further instructions. Manfred took this opportunity to get steaming drunk. I watched him stagger from table to table, face redder than ever, shirt straining over his distended belly. I could almost hear his shirt buttons screaming for help. I left Manfred cursing and shouting at some poor hapless Colombian in Teutonic Spanish, and slipped out with Maye for a Mexican meal.

I was in the old centre awaiting further orders, my bike was out of town in Pie de la Popa in Manfred's garage, and the *Clara E* was rusting away in its sleazy little port waiting for the green light. I stayed in an overpriced hotel. At $32 it might not seem expensive, but its equivalent in England would cost about £50, and you would not expect in an English £50 hotel to be greeted by an unshaven obese man wearing a dirty vest. Neither would you reasonably expect to find two large cockroaches in your bed.

Manfred, Davies (his handling agent) and I met the following morning at the Departamento Adminastrativo de Seguridad (DAS) to start the paper-chase of collecting the various documents I would need. Ever-mindful of the passage of drugs from Cartagena to Colon, the authorities run a fine-toothed comb over every scrap of paper (and they make sure you need plenty) that you possess. After spending the best part of the day in various government offices, I followed Manfred on the bike to the port, stopping to pick up some plastic sheeting on the way.

I stared disconsolately at the three long planks set at a 40° angle from the quayside to the boat adjacent to the *Clara E*. How the hell was I going to get a 250kg bike up there? There were enough men around to help, but where would they stand? The men fastened ropes and nylon straps to the headstock and crashbars, the idea being that two could pull, one would push and a man either side would supposedly steady it. And where would I go? I was given the

With Manfred, shipping agent, and helpers
– ready to get me on board the good ship *Clara E*

task of sitting on the bike and steering it. Frankly, I would rather have tried bungee jumping (I hate heights) than have attempted this madness.

The call was given to take the strain. Edwards, the huge, strong-as-an-ox first mate was pulling so effectively that the bike was lurching to one side. I fought to correct it – just one inch too far and both the bike and myself would be in the Atlantic, my dream ended. We inched up the plank at an agonisingly slow pace. Four metres felt like a mile. My T-shirt was drenched with perspiration, my mouth dry as I shouted out instructions: "Izquierda! ... Tiren!" Left ... Wait ... I was so agitated, I could not find the Spanish words.

We paused for breath once on board the first vessel. Now it was simply a matter of navigating the bike along a series of planks across the first ship and over the connecting plank between the two vessels. Even now, when I look back on that episode my stomach churns.

Maye came along with Manfred and Davies to wave me off. It was all quite pleasant, drifting away from port on that hot, sultry, star-filled night, watching the twinkling lights of the harbour and adjacent container ships receding into the distance. Little boys followed us on home-made rafts, shouting excitedly until eventually there was nobody – just me, the small crew and three hard days ahead.

Chapter 15

Nautical Nightmares and Scary Cities

I whiled away the evening in fitful sleep, naked, save for a mosquito net, my body bathed in sweat. The gentle sea breeze through the porthole did nothing to dissipate the suffocating heat of the cabin. I wanted to go up on deck for some air, but was reluctant to leave a cabin that didn't even have a door that would close, let alone a lock. I was sure the crew was honest but I did not want to put it to the test. Captain Felix promised to put a padlock on the door in the morning.

The *Clara E* was a Dutch-built coastal freighter. After entering the world in 1958, no doubt to be used in the Dutch Antilles, she has been passed down to increasingly impecunious owners. The members of the crew were all islanders, with the exception of one Colombian mainlander. The aforementioned Edwards, a 250lb powerhouse was clearly the Captain's most trusted crew member. A shy and socially awkward man, he nonetheless had the kind of calm, unruffled personality that takes everything in its stride. Jimmy, a polite, affable islander was my personal favourite. His face was ebony, exaggerating the whiteness of his gleaming teeth, prominently displayed by a permanent grin. He would show me photos of his teenage girlfriend. His mission in life was to save enough money while at sea, so he could marry her and buy a little grocery store on Providencia for the two of them. He would paint a vista of how wonderful their life was going to be together – I truly hope his dreams are realised. The ship's cook, Victor, lived in Colon. Born of a fourth generation English settler and a native black islander, the Captain referred to him as "English", though I can think of at least 58 million Britons who would not understand a word he was saying. He had brought along his heavily pregnant wife, Eloise and little boy. Eloise looked to be enjoying herself as much as me. Victor's filthy, unshaven appearance and frequent tendency to expectorate did not make me yearn to sample his cuisine. A month's worth of grime and diesel could be seen under his fingernails.

I had brought along some provisions but knew they were unlikely to last more than a day. Having seen the inside of the fridge, which made me gag, I decided to store them in my cabin. It came as no surprise to find a sticky, melted morass the following day.

The ship pitched around a lot that night, resulting in a broken indicator on the bike. Captain Felix helped me protect it from further damage with old carpet and foam.

I contemplated the thought of Colon, our port of arrival. Twenty years previously when working on the cruise liner, *S.S. Canberra*, I remembered docking in Cristobal, the adjacent port on the opposite bank of the mouth of the Panama Canal. The ship's passengers were advised strongly against going ashore, such was its reputation for violence and crime. I recalled going ashore at night with a gang of thirty other crew members – safety in numbers. I wouldn't have that luxury this time round. It said in my guidebook "A visit to a bank in Colon will most definitely be followed by a mugging". My recollections were of dilapidated wooden buildings with broad verandas, endless slum barrios and more brothels than I had ever seen in one town.

The grime of the *Clara E* cannot be overstated. I would put a clean white T-shirt on in my cabin, climb the few yards up to the hatch and arrive in the mess room with one black T-shirt. A visit to the ship's shower room and toilet, a fetid hole, was unthinkable. Despite my strong environmentalist views I resolved to dispose of all waste product through the porthole – my apologies to any beach-goers who stumble across a strangely coloured 7-Up bottle.

Captain Felix sat down at the mess table (where I spent the majority of my day) and informed me of a long delay due to prevailing head winds. The cook handed him two paper napkins, one for his lunch, another as a coaster for his drink. He flung the second one back at poor Victor with a torrent of abuse about wastage, pausing only to blow his nose on his T-shirt, thus saving further extravagance. Watching the smirks on the crew's faces, I guessed this was a frequent scenario. The Captain picked up the machete that he kept under the mess room table and leant over to me, whispering conspiratorially: "Am gonna sacrifice one of dem boys for lunch!"

Three days after leaving Cartagena, the coastline of Panama came into view. My relief was immense but was to be short-lived. We anchored out a couple of miles from the harbour awaiting a message on the radio from the port authority that we could dock and unload. The message never came. The crew had diligently scrubbed the ship down and painted the bridge ready for inspection, and had now settled in for the big wait. By lunchtime, all hell had broken loose. The Captain was informed that the primary gear for the lifting equipment had seized and would not function. The first engineer was responsible for the maintenance and safety checks of all such equipment. "Where that sonabitch! Am gonna chop his toes off," bawled Captain Felix, making chopping motions with his machete. Judging by his mood, it wouldn't end at the hapless engineer's toes.

Through lunch the Captain's mood had not changed. "What this fuckin' shit, man?" "That good Danish food Cap'n," replied the cook, who, after working on a Danish ship thirty years ago considered all things Danish to be the finest in the world. "Well, I say it shit!" snarled the Captain. I had to agree that gizzards, red beans and rice would not be my first choice and it's certainly not very Danish.

The pilot eventually came out to us with even bleaker news. Firstly, the port authority was not happy that the ship was carrying a passenger and, secondly, they were deeply involved with two other vessels, on one of which they'd found a cache of arms aboard, on the other a consignment of drugs. I was told it would be impossible to process me through Customs that afternoon (Saturday) and the Customs Shed would not be re-opening until Monday. I felt like screaming with frustration. I was due to meet up with my friend Louise in San Jose, Costa Rica the following night and knew, even after the bureaucratic nightmare of getting myself and the bike cleared, I still needed three days to get to San Jose.

The bike was not going anywhere for the next two days, but fortunately I was. I managed to get a seaman's pass allowing me to go into Colon for a little R & R. That is, if the possibility of having a knife held to one's throat could be described as 'recreational'. I took a taxi into town with Victor and Eloise. I had been told the Hotel Sotero was the best of a bad bunch and was determined not to spend the night on the ship. I had not been able to wash for four days and the promise of a shower and a proper bed was irresistible.

Victor, the cook, his wife Eloise and son

A tropical downpour did nothing to alleviate Colon's grim-ness. After checking into the Hotel Sotero, I darted a couple of blocks to a Chinese restaurant, trying always to keep within view of the police officers guarding the main street. I'm not easily frightened, but Colon is a challenge to even the most seasoned and worldly-wise traveller.

Colon developed as the northern terminus of the now-defunct Panama railroad which crossed from coast to coast. Completed in 1855, the railroad was extensively used by gold-rush speculators heading to California from the east coast of the USA. That might sound like a massive detour but it certainly beat being ambushed by hostile Indians in America's heartlands. Colon became a pros-perous city, though only for as long as it took the USA to build a trans-continental railroad shortly after.

In the early 1880s, the French began to build the Panama Canal. Four years later, a Colombian arsonist, trying to precipitate a revo-lution, practically burned the whole city down, requiring the French to rebuild it – which they did in a French colonial style. The wooden structures still exist today, though in a greatly deteriorated state. Colon's second major economic blow occurred when the long-awaited Canal was completed. The thousands of workers

drafted in to build the Canal became unemployed overnight.
Nowadays Colon merely services the needs of sailors – mainly their
sexual needs, as they await passage through the Canal, metaphori-
cally speaking.

There are a large number of Chinese in Colon, descendants of
the Chinese labourers who helped build the railroad. I pondered
this fact over a fairly disgusting chow mein.

I had arranged to go for a beer with two of the crew members of
the *Clara E*. This became expensive as numerous bar girls tried to
squeeze drinks out of us while my 'friends' tried to side-step picking up their bar tabs. I soon wised up to this, closing my own bills to
the nearest balboa – the local currency.

My basic little hotel room felt like the Ritz after the *Clara E*. I
stood in the shower for a full 20 minutes luxuriating in the novelty
of running water. Captain Felix expressed a preference for the
Hotel Sotero. Over one of his mess room homilies he told me how
he liked to "sex dem bitches up" while residing at the hotel. I had
resolved to keep my virtue and wallet intact, and had an early
night.

I decided that two nights at the Sotero was too extravagant so
returned to the *Clara E* with a cold six-pack for a night in the mess
room. I certainly didn't go short on entertainment. Captain Felix
decided he was going to re-enact all of his most noteworthy first
fights for me – right there in the 7' x 5' room. Between parries,
lunges and expletives directed at his imaginary opponent, he told
me of the newsreels he would watch of Cassius Clay and how, as a
youth, he would model himself on him.

On a more serious note, he told me of the two years he had spent
in Memphis state penitentiary as an unwilling guest of Uncle Sam.
Drugs, smuggled on one of his ships had been discovered by the
Drugs Enforcement Agency (DEA). Of the twelve crew, nobody
would own up – even though it was clearly the work of one individual. The American judicial system, not known for their objectivity
on the subject of drugs, simply threw all twelve of them into jail for
nine years. After two years, in the light of new evidence, Captain
Felix and ten of the crew were pardoned while the true culprit
remained incarcerated. Captain Felix received no compensation
for this travesty of justice.

He recounted another sad story of how he lost his eldest son at
the age of thirty-three in a diving accident. It affected Captain Felix

profoundly. I realised that behind the gruff façade lay a decent, kind-hearted man. I was going to miss the old boy. His oddball personality and complete disregard for political correctness was rather engaging.

I awoke at the crack of dawn and we set about unloading the bike in a manner that was only slightly less-nerve wrecking than four days before. I set about the tedious task of taking taxis from ramshackle immigration office to Customs Shed and sundry other bureaucracies before having my belongings examined with a fine-toothed comb. Fired up from their guerilla arms discovery a couple of days before, Customs were being extra vigilant. I had hired a 'Tramite" to help navigate me through Customs procedures as quickly as possible. Despite the modest cost, I usually liked to perform these tasks myself. But this time, I simply had to get back on the road at the earliest opportunity.

Chapter 16

Ashley Rhodes 1, Panama Highway Patrol 0

The 74 kilometres from Colon to Panama City was like passing from Lagos to L.A. – for here was a bright shiny city that looked as though it might be going somewhere. Panama City has a strong North American feel as result of the US's long involvement in Panama's political history – not an arrangement the Panamanians were ever very keen on. Interestingly, although the balboa is Panama's official currency, it's only available in coin form. They do their banknote transactions in US dollar bills.

Just outside Panama City, a truck jack-knifed right in front of me. As it lay in a ditch on its side, trailer savagely twisted, I fully expected the driver to be badly hurt. Thankfully, he was O.K. Carnage on the roads is a way of life in Latin America, eliciting a weary resignation by public and officialdom alike.

The long straight road north of Panama City cuts a swathe through a broad savannah and is punctuated by small US style towns, nestling in an abundance of greenery. I took the good condition of the road as an opportunity to make rapid progress, flashing past long lines of slow-moving lumber trucks. My progress was clearly a little too fast for the police motorcyclist who flagged me down. Dismounting from his antediluvian Chinese motorcycle he stretched to his full 5' 7" and proceeded to admonish me about the danger of overtaking on solid lines. I dropped into unilingual gringo mode with the hope of frustrating him and escaping with a verbal caution. He was persistent and demanded my driving licence which he would take to the local fixed penalty officer from where I could collect it in three days. There was no way I was about to surrender my real licence, so after establishing he didn't speak a word of English, I gave him my cycle speedway racing licence, which looks similar to a US-style driver's licence. Then came the sting; I could avoid all this 'inconvenience' if I gave him $20 now. I told him that I would be more than happy to collect my (cycle speedway) licence in three days but thanked him for the offer and rode off grinning like a Cheshire Cat.

*   *   *   *

Deep in Kuna Indian territory it began to go dark. I had foolishly imagined a country as small as Panama would be well served with petrol stations. With only a thimbleful of fuel left and no signs of civilization ahead, I realised this was not the case. With about two kilometres left in my tank I stumbled across a lumber yard that agreed to sell me a couple of Pepsi bottles of fuel.

Just 54 kilometres short of the Costa Rican border lies the town of David, a pleasant, orderly little town that was to be my base that night, where the comfortable Hotel Castilla awaited me and a well-earned *ceviche* and grilled calamares at a nearby fish restaurant.

A detour from the Panamericana the following morning cost me greatly. I had decided to try and find some Kuna Indian settlements, so selected a twisting country road of exquisite beauty with picture-perfect little *fincas* nestling in exotic foliage. Bright yellow butterflies danced in my path. All was well with the world. I stopped a Kuna lady for directions. She told me I could cross the border further north at La Serena, saving considerable time.

La Serena was passed with no evidence of a border. After another hour's riding and still no border, I doubled back to La Serena and embarked on a frustrating search for the mysteriously absent aforementioned. I eventually found it – a one-man hut. Duly stamped out I went in search of the Costa Rican Customs and Immigration post. There wasn't one. This meant heading down the same road on which I'd just done a two-hour loop. Angry and rattled, I turned up at the Panamericana border control. Having wasted the thick end of four hours I was still only 54 kilometres from the town of David where I had spent the previous night. What was more, the drizzle of the late morning had turned into a downpour of hurricane proportions. I presented myself at Immigration looking like some kind of amphibious creature – water overflowing from the top of my boots and supposedly waterproof gloves inflated like water balloons. Due to some perverse emigration law, or more likely the intransigence of the worthless specimen who sat before me, I was told that as I had been stamped out in La Serena, I would have to exit the country from there. I felt the red mist rise. I was going nowhere – certainly not for an unnecessary 75-minute detour in the direction from where I had just come (twice) in monsoon conditions. I steadfastly refused to move from his window until he brought that rubber stamp onto my passport. Grudgingly, he eventually did so.

The Costa Rican border was equally frustrating in a different way. I spent an hour filling in form after endless form while a cheerful little chappie intoxicated with his official status sent me on endless trips to a photocopier while he sat in his nice dry office. When he had relieved me of large amounts of money and done everything short of genetically fingerprinting me, I was eventually allowed into Costa Rica.

Despite the driving rain, it was clear to see that Costa Rica lived up to its Garden of Eden image with wall-to-wall rain forest. Like Panama, it has a strong feel of the USA. The 'Ticos' as the Costa Ricans are known are generally plumper than in other Latin American countries and favour the Nike-and-Bermuda-shorts-look beloved of North Americans.

I stopped at a roadside restaurant where I headed straight for the men's room, undressed, wrung out my sodden T-shirt and underwear which were so wet the colours had run. The next six hours were a living hell as I battled against dense fog at a lethargic crawl. My feet had been so wet for so long I would not have been surprised if I'd developed trench foot.

By the time I reached San Jose I hadn't the enthusiasm to find the only pre-booked hotel of my trip. The Hotel Edelweiss was located within a maze of one-way streets, and mindful of the fact that Louise had probably been hanging around all day waiting for me, I did not want to prolong the wait. I gave a taxi driver a dollar to lead me there. I was delighted to find out she had only arrived five minutes earlier herself.

A bad head-cold kept me under the weather for a few days and unable to enjoy the pleasures of San Jose, not that it had too much to offer. A lot of its colonial architecture had been flattened by earthquakes and what replaced it could hardly be called inspiring. It reminded me of a small 1960s American city. I took the opportunity of a three-day break to get the bike serviced at Euromotors, the

With Max Soto, customer service manager at Euro Autos de Centro America, San Jose

local BMW dealer, where Max, the service manager, really put himself out for me. Short on staff, he did the tyre change and service himself and rode down to the Hotel Edelweiss to give me regular progress reports. Having worn out my original Metzelers, then Bridgestones, I chose Dunlops this time (actually I was not given a choice). I planned to try Michelins next, so I could compare all of the factory recommended tyres back-to-back.

Louise and I quickly tired of San Jose, having decided that the best the city had to offer was the band, which played at the bandstand in the park. This was a view shared by Hans, the owner of the Edelweiss, though he was rather less charitable in his viewpoint. He saw it as a once prosperous city that had stagnated due to a 'lazy' workforce who were fonder of calling strikes than working. He felt their Catholic faith was their only driving force. I failed to see why that should be any obstacle to productivity but he was adamant. Wondering why he had not packed his bags and headed back to the Fatherland, he told me that he owned several small businesses that would be difficult to dispose of.

After much debate, we decided that five days relaxation in the small surfers' resort of Tamarindo would do us both good. Louise would pick up a flight and I, naturally, would ride there. But what would normally have been a pleasant four-hour ride on decent tarmac to Tamarindo felt like an eternity, my eyes streaming, head woolly with catarrh. I took a detour to visit a serpent farm, which looked promising, but could not bring myself to stump up the ridiculous $11 entry fee – the price of a decent hotel room in Costa Rica. Two French guys pulled up behind me in a jeep. They felt the same way. We asked if we could skip the 45-minute guided tour and just pay $15 for the three of us. Despite the fact there was not a soul in the place, our offer was refused. I was beginning to understand Hans's point of view.

Arriving in Liberia, just short of Tamarindo, I stopped at a crossroads to dig out the address of the B & B where I was due to meet Louise. Cursing myself, I realised that in my befuddled state, I had left the details in San José. There are twenty-plus accommodations in Tamarindo. I could not even remember the name of the place having only half listened when Louise read excerpts from the *Footprint* guide to me. I was going to have to find and visit them one by one.

Tamarindo is basically a one-dirt-road town the main street of which runs parallel to the beach. Its hostelries however are usually located down long dirt lanes in the interests of privacy. In the energy-sapping afternoon humidity I trudged around each and every one. "Señorita Ross?" No – move on. After numerous blind alleys I eventually found her at the Villa Alegre, a secluded B and B nestling in a thicket close to a small cove. Louise had not disappointed me with her choice. A charming oasis of tranquillity, Barry and Susie, the retired Californian owners, ran it like a Swiss watch with meticulous eye for detail. A bear of a man with snow-white hair and a permanent genial smile, Barry prides himself on being able to produce 21 different breakfasts without duplicating one. Louise had a big crush on him – in a father-daughter kind of way. I think it was mutual.

Lounging by the pool sipping Chardonnay and nibbling Barry's legendary *bocas* (bite-sized pre-dinner appetizers) while Louise hunted for seashells on the beach, was all very pleasant, as was staying in the country-themed spacious bedrooms. Mine was in 'Guatemala'. However, I was becoming soft. I yearned for the excitement of war zones, corrupt officials and Third World hardships. I knew I would not want for much in my next destination – Nicaragua.

Barry and I drove Louise to Tamarindo's tiny airstrip from

where she would fly to San Jose and connect with an international flight. The airstrip boasted little but a small Piper aircraft, a disused hut and a gaggle of surly officials. Passengers added up to a bunch of sun-bleached surfers clutching their boards, a wizened Scandinavian woman, who had OD'd on ultra violet rays many years ago, and her pet chimpanzee, proudly strutting around in his diapers, thoughtfully provided for the benefit of the other passengers.

I was the only guest left at the Villa Alegre. It was too late in the day to resume my journey so I spent an extra night there. Trying hard to give Barry and Susie some rare privacy, I wandered into town for dinner, navigating the pitch-black trails with my torch. Iguanas and crabs scuttled for cover in the beam of my torch, bats swooped in my path alarmingly. Dinner was an unmitigated disaster. The rule of "no shoes, no service" doesn't apply in Costa Rican towns as it does in coastal North America. Not having sun-bleached hair cascading down my back or wearing cut-off denims, a Hawaiian shirt and an ethnic talisman around my neck, I soon became invisible to the waitress. She eventually served me, barely concealing a yawn and giving me the "I'd rather be surfing" treatment. I responded at the end of the (poor) meal by showering her with profuse gratitude for the wonderful service I had received and simultaneously deleting the 'optional' service charge from the bill.

After one of Barry's special breakfasts (being the only guest entitled me to 'the works') I was sad to turn my back on Barry and Susie and their charming home, but somewhat relieved to escape the claustrophobic feel of Tamarindo.

Chapter 17

Lewd acts,
Christian Missionaries and
Mud-Wrestling – Honduras

The usual horde of kids gathered around me at the Nicaraguan border of Peñas Blancas, offering their services as
tramitadores (unofficial guides through the endless bureaucratic hurdles), change-givers and vehicle guards, the latter of
which I completely ignored ... to my cost. Riding between
Immigration and the Nicaraguan Customs area, my bike
developed a pronounced clicking noise, reminiscent of my
childhood, when we used to stick pieces of card in the back
wheels of our pushbikes that would catch against the spokes
making an interesting sound effect. Except this time it wasn't
card catching against the swinging arm, but a six inch nail
which had been driven into my new rear tyre – clearly an act of
vandalism from a disenchanted child hustler. I quickly
considered my options. The nail was perilously close to the
sidewall, meaning that if I pulled the nail out the tyre could
deflate leaving it not repairable. I didn't fancy my chances of
finding the correct-sized tyre in Nicaragua. The nail was so far
in that its tip was showing through on the other side. I crossed
my fingers and eased it out with my pliers. Miraculously,
nothing happened. I expected a slow puncture at the very
least but it seemed that the deep tread blocks of the Dunlops
had saved me. The nail had merely pierced the tread block and
exited the other side, leaving the tyre carcass undamaged.
Counting my blessings I entered Central America's largest
republic, a country blighted by Civil War, earthquakes and
volcanic eruptions.

The 1978-79 revolution by the left-wing Sandanista guerilla
movement against the Somoza Government resulted in a lengthy,

US-supported civil war, which in turn had caused a rapid disintegration of the country's infrastructure that had persisted since the 1980s. A lengthy US trade embargo did not help and, despite a return to peace in the early 1990s, Nicaragua still bears the social and physical scars of its bloody past. There was also the devastation left by Hurricane Mitch and El Niño, with over 30,000 casualties and extensive property damage – particularly noticeable in the once-elegant old mansions I passed on my approach into Managua, a number of which were missing their roofs. All this has conspired to give Nicaragua's tourist board one big nightmare after another and the country now has the lowest per capita income in Latin America.

After a scenic ride past Nicaragua's long volcanic chain I approached Managua, the capital which lies on the banks of the huge 8,264 sq km Lake Managua. I had ordered a couple of fresh visors for my Arai helmet from England. These were to be sent by Federal Express to be picked up by me at the Hotel Intercontinental. I had given that address as the only hotel I remembered from my trip to Managua four years previously that would be unlikely to lose the package or perform some similar cock-up. In the event, it was FedEx which managed to cock-up quite nicely by sending the visors to the wrong country. I would have to ride through three more countries with badly scratched visors before picking them up in Belize.

I decided to stay in the Intercontinental. Though expensive, it is conveniently located in a city with a rather strange layout. The centre of Managua was devastated by an earthquake in 1931 and again in 1972. As a result, the centre is now in ruins – an area of wasteland dominated by the ruins of the Cathedral. The new 'centre' is shared between the area where the Intercontinental stands and a ribbon development on the four-lane Carratera a Masaya.

Managua doesn't exactly have a host of tourist attractions. I visited the Palacio Nacional and the Cathedral, which lie side-by-side at the epicentre of the earthquake zone. Despite the East End bombsite location, the Palacio is a pristine and rather splendid building. I could not see the wisdom in pouring millions of dollars from already depleted coffers into a building that sat on the site of 16 seismic fault lines.

On my previous visit to Managua I had stayed at a far more

modest hotel just around the corner from the Intercontinental. I recalled a gang of three prostitutes who used to hang out on the corner between the two hotels. As I used to walk up the hill towards my favourite restaurant they would engage me in banter. One thing really stuck in my mind. There was one girl in particular who told me that her sole reason for being 'on the game' was to finance the epilepsy drugs that her young son required. There were few regular jobs that would pay enough to cover these astronomical items. I decided to find her. With my connections at the David Lewis Centre for Epilepsy I may have been able to source cheaper drugs for her, or at the very least, I could help generate some press interest in the plight of others in a similar situation.

I trudged up and down the Avenida, speaking to every working girl I came across. I did not even know her name so had to rely on a description of her personal circumstances. Nothing. Furthermore, I don't think some of the girls viewed my interest as entirely altruistic. I was forced to give up.

I retired to the ice-cold air-conditioned luxury of the Intercontinental. The hotel shop sold high quality export cigars and coffee. Nicaragua produces both items to a very high standard, though if one orders a coffee just about anywhere it tastes like a bad cup of 1950s Camp Coffee Essence. Anything of quality is exported to the gringos. No wonder the Nicaraguans harbour resentments.

Packing my belongings I suddenly made a terrible discovery. A discovery that made my heart sink and made me feel sick with worry. Everything, from my passport to my bike ownership documents and insurance certificate, had gone

Everything was at stake. Being in a country like Nicaragua, I did not rate too highly the chances of recouping my losses, so went on an all-out offensive to track them down. I phoned the border control and offered anonymity and a substantial reward to anyone who could produce them. I did the same at the hotel, circulating the message through the concierge and front desk. By this time there were not many Nicaraguans left in the country who were unaware of my plight. You can therefore imagine my embarrassment (and delight) when I opened my secret hiding place in my bag and found the folder of documents lying there unmolested. I cursed myself for my stupidity, gave Jaime, the head receptionist, a generous tip for practically having turned the entire hotel upside down, mumbled my apologies and gratitude ... and fled!

Opting for the Panamericana rather than the road across the Sierra Managua, I quickly arrived in Leon, only 88 kilometres from Managua. A fine old colonial town, Leon would have made an interesting overnight stay, but with some time to make up I just spent an hour relaxing in the pleasant, shaded Parque Jerez. Lying, as it does, at the foot of some impressive volcanoes and with an air of decay and faded colonialism, Leon was for me the quintessential Central American town.

I remembered from before that the Nicaragua-Honduras border was a tough one. It was going to be a lot tougher with my bike in tow. The border officials did not disappoint me. I started the procedure without the help of a *tramitadore* but by the time I'd been to six different offices and watched six unshaven 'officials' type worthless documents on antiquated Adler typewriters, I soon capitulated. The dissimilarity between the fees and procedure I experienced and that laid down in the *Footprint* guidebook I was using had nothing to do with the guide's reliability and everything to do with their frame of mind on the night. $40 is a ludicrous amount to pay to enter any country and in inverse proportion to the tiny size of the Republic of Honduras.

I had noticed when riding through Nicaragua that many of their roads and bridges bore signs testifying to the funding they had received from countries as diverse as Norway and Japan, while many of Honduras's main stretches of roads had been built and funded by the USA. It struck me that they must have some great negotiators, when the UK struggles to get money from the EEC.

Under an ink-black sky on the lonely outskirts of Choluteca lay El Camino Real, a nondescript motel by a nondescript town. The bellboy escorted me to my room, his machine-gun tucked under his arm. In my hot, weary state I was unperturbed by the small creatures scampering across the floor or, for that matter, the miniature reptile occupying the shower tray. I heaved myself onto the bed, fully clothed, and fell into a deep sleep.

Lingering over breakfast – the Camino Real's answer to French toast – I pored over my map, trying to find a direct road to Belize. I discovered that Belize, which once belonged to Guatemala, doesn't share a land border with Honduras. Due to the paucity of roads, I would be better tracking the Pacific coast route, even though my destination (Belize) lay on the Caribbean coast.

I gunned the bike down the shimmering road to Tegucigalpa,

holding a steady 90mph, the molten tarmac and fertile pastureland flashing past me. Today I was going to make some progress.

I broke the ride to Tegucigalpa at a small sleepy village, which I chose as a likely place for good 'hot photography'. I had been taking photos of national headwear ever since leaving Chile and remembered from a previous trip to Copan that Hondurans wear a type of Stetson-cum-Panama. I remember trying to buy one, thinking what a hit it would be in Wilmslow. After trying on about 86 Honduran hats I realised that not only did I look a complete pillock, but clearly no-one in Honduras had a head as big as mine.

It was a friendly village and its elder statesman posed gamely for my artistic shots.

*   *   *   *

I bypassed Tegucigalpa, shuddering at my recollections of this crime-ridden polluted city. I had somewhat foolishly signed up for a 'gentleman's tour' of the fleshpots of Tegucigalpa, where we were shuttled from bordello to bordello – a friend and I, along with six other lecherous characters. The evening culminated in Dwight, an obese one-legged American, removing his artificial leg to perform a 'lewd act' with two Honduran prostitutes in the confines of an 8ft x 8ft windowless room with cockroaches scampering across the floor. I felt unclean for at least a week.

Skirting the heavy industrial pallor that hangs over Tegucigalpa, I climbed into the fresher pine-scented mountain air on a road that would eventually take me to the coastal city of San Pedro Sula, some 285 kilometres away.

San Pedro Sula is regarded as the fastest-growing city between Mexico and Panama. I checked into the Holiday Inn, which was overflowing with Southern Baptists from Alabama on a 'mission'. The receptionists were dealing with their impossible requests with good grace, indulging them like small children. One woman with a particularly astringent voice refused to go up in the lift unless accompanied by a member of staff. I kept a low profile hoping I would not be confused for one of them. San Pedro Sula did not have much to offer beyond a good seafood restaurant that did a great *ceviche*. I decided to leave for Guatemala in the morning.

I hung around in San Pedro till lunchtime waiting for my camera to be repaired. Still, it's worth the wait when you know that the alternative in England would be "scrap it and buy a new one". In Latin America if it's repairable you can bet your life they'll fix it.

I planned to head for the Guatemalan border and if I reached Flores, so much the better. Trying to find a more direct route to Belize City, I stopped at Puerto Cortes from where I was told I could get a sailing to Guatemala, though after extensive enquiries I discovered it would most likely be on some kind of canoe which was bound to sink under the weight of the bike, plus the fishermen who operated the service worked to a very loose schedule. The road route via Omoa seemed the only option and looked to be an increasingly attractive one as I sped through lush jungle with a palm-fringed shoreline to my right. However, payback time came all too soon as the road rapidly deteriorated.

I forded two rivers without too much difficulty, but my heart sank as I came to an abrupt halt at the edge of a stretch of road that had been turned into a thick bog. A truck was buried in the quagmire up to its axles with another truck valiantly trying to pull it out and failing miserably. The quagmire stretched for about 50 metres with no visible areas of traction to be seen. There was no alternative route that did not involve a 100-plus kilometre detour – and that was an optimistic guess. I decided to give it a go.

I felt like Evel Knievel must have felt before a big jump. I couldn't judge how deep the mud was and knew my road tyres would offer me no assistance. I accelerated towards it, back tyre slewing from side to side, up into second ... plop! I sank like a stone with thick glutinous mud up to the tops of my wheels. I desperately tried to keep the momentum, feathering the clutch ... third gear. No chance! I slowly sank, unable to do anything but watch the slimy mud crawl up my leather-clad legs. I vainly tried to power myself out, but only succeeded in digging myself in deeper. The first whiffs of frying clutch plate told me to stop. A bunch of small boys were giggling at the sight of this Power Ranger-type gringo on his space-age motorcycle foundering in the mud like a bathing hippopotamus. Someone went to fetch some rope which they secured to each crash bar. It took three men each side, along with me burning my clutch, to haul it out. Thanking them profusely, I sought directions to Honduran Immigration which was just an hour's ride up the road – with, apparently, no more bogs.

The border post was just a small clearing in the jungle with two small huts in which lolled the inevitable officials with their pre-war typewriters. Looking like a mud wrestler, I asked a money-changer if he knew of somewhere I could sluice the worst of the mud from my trousers and boots. Directed to a stone trough of water I happily set about washing some of the mud away until the water in the trough was the colour of pondwater. Suddenly, a woman marched out of the adjacent hut and launched a string of obscenities at me. She lambasted me for a full five minutes while a group of men stood watching, convulsed with laughter. To my horror and embarrassment I realised I had been cleaning myself in the poor woman's fresh water supply!

Ater 15 kilometres down a single track dirt road I arrived at Guatemalan Immigration and Customs – a more isolated and basic version of its Honduran counterpart, if that is at all possible. I'm used to being treated as anything ranging from a mild irritant to a figure of contempt by most Latin American border officials, despite some notable exceptions. It came as no small surprise to be greeted with the utmost respect and to be addressed as "Mr Rhodes" by the immigration official in this remote outpost. After he had formally welcomed me to Guatemala he informed me that, although Immigration could process me, Customs had packed up and gone home ten minutes previously. Judging by our isolation, 'home' might be some distance. He offered to type up the vehicle entry form himself. Ah! So here was the sting ... I sensed his next words would be ... "for a fee". He set to work on a typewriter which broke new ground in antiquity. He then cajoled his lazy colleagues into putting their stamps on it, all of whom would have clearly preferred to carry on smoking and chatting in the shade of the tree under which they were congregated. They gradually acquiesced in order to humour their zealous colleague. The bribe never happened ... I'd actually met the only enthusiastic bureaucrat in Latin America. I told him so.

Chapter 18

Bite-sized Britain – Belize

It was turning dark in an area renowned for its banditry and Flores was still a good four hours away. The remote gas station that I stopped at had a veritable arsenal of decommissioned armaments ready for an inevitable attack. I recalled the stories of a tour group I had flown out to meet in Guatemala City three years previously. The day before I had met up with them, their bus had been held up by armed bandits in the region where I now was. The bandits had relieved them of all their possessions at gunpoint ... in broad daylight.

The next village of any size was Rio Dulce, a place that has unfortunately become a minor tourist attraction due to its beautiful jungle settling and the adjacent Lago de Izabel. Fortunately, tourism brings hotels and, with the onset of another downpour, I was ready for one. I found the Vinas del Lago, a small eco-hotel nestling in the undergrowth, alive with the screeching of bullfrogs and parrots. After a very large Garifuna[1] lady had cooked me dinner in a nearby straw hut I fell into a long and dreamless sleep.

The rain pounded at my window relentlessly. I knew it was going to last the day, so saw no point in hanging around. I wasted the first hour trudging around in the rain looking for some mystical character called Mario, who I was told was the only man around who could change my Honduran *limpera* into Guatemalan *quetzals*. I knew from experience, the further one moves away from the border, the harder it is to change the previous country's currency.

The road north to Tikal greeted me with many glimpses of everyday Guatemalan life. Families washing themselves ... and their trucks ... in picturesque meandering rivers, a wedding taking place under a tarpaulin pitched in a wooded copse. I don't know what the

---

1

Black communities living on the Caribbean coast of Central America

guests made of a strange, Gore-Tex-clad man crashing through the undergrowth with zoom-lens in hand hoping for a "Hello!" type exclusive.

As I moved away from the small settlements, the road became a dead-straight ribbon cutting a swathe through the jungle. A sky-filling black cloud swept towards me. In the absence of anywhere to take cover and don my waterproofs, I decided to hope that it would pass. It didn't. I felt as though the Mayan gods were visiting some terrible misfortune on those who dared to venture through their sacred lands. I squirmed in discomfort as chill water penetrated my 'waterproof' trousers and bathed my nether regions. As all bikers know, this is the point where it's wise to give up. I followed a long waterlogged dirt trail to the encouragingly luxurious-sounding 'Westin Hotel Camino Real Tikal'. I cleared a path to the front desk, where I stood in a rapidly expanding puddle. The receptionist, with a barely concealed look of distaste, moved my sodden gloves and a now brown (previously yellow and silver) Arai helmet to one side. I sensed she would rather be arranging lake cruises for Hawaiian-shirted gringos. I eyed the serene lake of Peten Itza beyond the hotel's gardens and almost wished I was one ... but not for long.

I awoke at the crack of dawn, eager to experience Tikal before the hordes arrived. I duly presented myself at the gates to this man-made phenomenon, tingling with anticipation ... just to find out there was no petrol available ahead. I guess they had little need for unleaded in AD300. This meant doubling back for a 45-kilometre round trip to hunt out some old timer who sold bottles of petrol from his front room. Frustratingly, I had lost my time advantage and by the time I returned the mini-buses of goggle-eyed punters were lining up.

This ancient Mayan site with a total 'urban' area of 100 square kilometres falls short of Machu Picchu only in the sense that it was built in a more accessible location. Tikal is indeed very impressive with 1,400 year-old pyramids to clamber over and the Mundo Perdido (lost world) where toucans, howler monkeys and a wide range of obscure bird and animal life can be found. Trouble is, it's a case of "early bird catches the worm" and if you arrive as late as I did, the most interesting species you'll find is 'Germanus Backpackerus' – and plenty of them.

I walked away from it despising myself for having no more soul and imagination than to view it as more than a bunch of old stones. On later reflection I tried to visualise it with the sun setting over those sacred stones ... or maybe bathed in the soft glow of moonlight with Mayans hunched around a huge fire ... and not a visitor centre or guided trail to be seen. I warmed to this image and decided I probably did have a soul after all.

*   *   *   *

Eventually, all my clothes were dry and I was free to check out of the Westin Tikal and do the three-hour hop to Belize City. I was curious about this tiny Caribbean nation. It would have been considerably quicker to avoid Belize altogether. Had I stuck with the Panamericana and avoided the eastern side of the Central American isthmus I could have saved several days, but this was not what the journey was about. I had made several other big diversions to see places that fascinated me. Belize was my first English-speaking country since arriving in the Americas. At the border I noticed a marked difference in style and atmosphere between Guatemala and Belize, interesting in that Belize was once part of Guatemala, though its claim to sovereignty was never fully recognised. The British, who had first come over from Jamaica in about 1640, along with their black slaves, made it a colony in 1864. It became a crown colony nine years later and did not declare its independence until as recently as 1981.

As I rode through lush rolling countryside, past fields of cattle, with my Belizean dollars in my pocket, proudly displaying the Queen's head, I had little doubt in my mind I was in an ex-colony; further confirmed in a bar I stopped at for a beer. Located in an isolated hamlet outside Belmopan, the diminutive capital, its walls were festooned with military regalia left by British troops who had been stationed locally. I absorbed myself for an hour reading the graffiti about what the Welsh Guards, among others, thought of Belize.

I like the names of the hamlets and villages: Roaring Creek, Gallon Jug, Hattieville. I flashed through Belmopan in an instant, although it is the administrative capital. Belize City is by far the larger city but with a population of 52,000 that is hardly vast.

I pulled into Belize City as night fell. The clapboard façades and iron roofs of the period houses that feature heavily in the city give it a strong atmosphere. I picked up a slight feel of Savannah, Georgia or a pre-refit Charleston, South Carolina. I checked into the Radisson St. George which had a charming receptionist called Deshawn with whom I was able to hang around and flirt – so far so good.

I soon realised that Belize was not quite so relaxed and easy going as I thought when I tried to take photos of a random selection of buildings, and was met with a tirade of abuse, some of it hurled from the balconies of buildings, other dark mutterings from passers-by. For the life of me I could not see my crime.

I met Debbie, a very engaging 'digger', in the bar of the Radisson. From Pennsylvania, she had joined a group of archaeologists currently carrying out an unpublicised excavation of a Mayan site, deep in the Guatemalan jungle. She and her digging accomplice, Debbie, were taking a few days R&R from the deprivations of jungle living. They invited me up-country to the site for a couple of days' digging, but rum punches beside the pool at the Radisson seemed preferable to snakebites and scorpion stings deep in the jungle. I think I've watched too much Indiana Jones.

I met up with Linda at 'Four, Fourth Street', a nice old colonial home that offered patio dining and great fish. It would have been perfect had the waitress not been in such a hurry to vacate the place that she held her hand out for every plate while I ate from it. Customers are treated like a huge nuisance in Belize – which is a shame, as much money has been invested to promote tourism. Interestingly, the majority of successful businesses are Chinese-run.

I chose the wrong route out of Belize City the following morning – no mean feat when there are only two roads out of town and you've got a detailed map to consult. This foolishness caused me a 70-mile detour and a return visit to Belize City an hour later.

At the Mexican border, I spotted a fully laden Yamaha 750 Tenere on French plates, with a chic-looking Frenchman (aren't they always?) sporting a neat little goatee beard and ultra-cool shades. Fabien told me he was about half-way through a round-the-world trip, confirmed by the well-worn off-road tyres he had strapped to the back of the bike. He had had a couple of bad experiences: an arrest in Vietnam, held up at gunpoint by a drug-crazed lunatic in Vladivostock who, it seems, undid his flies and waved his member at a terrified Fabien, while simultaneously flailing his other weapon (the gun) in the poor Frenchman's face and yelling at him in Russian. Fabien was a little confused as to what message he was trying to get across.

I suspected this might have been Fabien's worst day by far, but no ... with a contemptuous sneer he described his arrest at California's LA airport for a minor immigration irregularity. The indignant Frenchman was handcuffed and frog-marched around the airport in full view of all passengers. Feeling by this stage like the lowest form of human life, Fabien launched into an eloquent speech addressed to the police chief, his men and any passengers who happened to be passing. The thrust of his speech compared his treatment in the USA unfavourably to that he had received in any fascist, Marxist or third-world country you care to mention. He rounded his oration off with the assertion that the USA could never hope to attain the high standards of human rights enjoyed in France. The attendant officials did not propose to hold a healthy debate on the subject of the finest traditions of democracy. They did, however, slap a ten-year ban on his re-entering the country. This did not bother him unduly, other than the fact that he had cultivated relationships with several American girls whom he had photographed practically nude as a 'study' to "celebrate ze deeferent cultures of ze world". His hopes to re-visit them for further 'cultural exchanges' would now be dashed.

Chapter 19

Mexican Beauties, Zapatistas and Hairless Dogs

Mexico requires that owners of temporarily imported vehi-cles post a bond for the full value of the vehicle – some-thing like a Carnet de Passages. Would you be happy leaving an open credit card slip with a Mexican 'official'? I certainly wasn't.

I took a due-west course along the base of the Yucatan penin-sula. A 300-kilometre ride on a dead-straight road that cuts through a fertile plain. Escareega, a dusty little town servicing the through traffic of buses, looked the most promising overnight stop in this sparsely populated region. The only thing going for it is that it's cheap.

I decided the first taco stand had not given me enough tamales, so I gorged myself at a second stand, liberally dolloping hot sauce onto my tortillas from a grubby plastic bottle. The change of cuisine (if one can call it that) coupled with heartrending Mexican ballads blasting from tinny transistor radios confirmed I was defi-nitely in Mexico. I contemplated the unlikelihood of finding any decent food in these small Mexican towns and resigned myself to the prospect of an exclusive diet of maize pancakes wrapped around dry, shredded beef.

There's a zoo in Tuxtia Gutierrez which is said to be the finest in Mexico. As I wheeled the bike out of the courtyard of my dingy motel, I decided to make a large detour and see it for myself.

A vivid blue sky and a refreshing gentle breeze served to heighten the pleasure of my ride to the Chiapas border. The heavily wooded flanks of the road were alive with thousands of yellow butterflies. On occasions I would ride through a wall of them, a large number of which would end their lives splattered in a yellow carpet across my windscreen. Like most moments of undiluted pleasure in life, it did not last for long and soon I found myself at the Chiapas border being charged with an imaginary infraction of the law by a fresh-faced young policeman. I went on to the counter-attack by feigning indignation that he should try and extort money from a fellow officer of the law and that he should be ashamed of himself. After further clumsy attempts to extort money from me he said "OK, well, can you give me money for a Coke then?" Little wonder that Mexican police aren't top of your average Mexican's list of "people in whom we trust'.

As I forked off along the fertile valley route to Tuxtla, I began to consider the safety implications of the region I had just entered. I had always associated the Mexican revolutionary, Emiliano Zapata, with Jason King-style moustaches without being fully aware that the Ejercito Zapatista Liberacion Nacional (EZLN) that he spawned, had been involved in a civil war of some magnitude (60,000 Mexican troops involved) in the late nineties, a mere stone's throw away from the area I was approaching.

The war had been ignited principally by the Government's alleged disregard for the rights of indigenous peoples. Although no longer a war zone, a strong element of lawlessness still exists in the villages around San Crisobal de las Casas, namely robbery, rape, non-specific assault and other unpleasantness. My guidebook was peppered with warnings about the Chiapas region.

The mountains surrounding the valley where San Cristobal is sited are quite beautiful – lush, fertile agricultural land inhabited mainly by Indians. I spotted two pretty teenage girls dressed in tribal costume. I took them to be Tenejapa or Chamula, their multi-coloured hand-woven dresses were fringed in lace. Despite all the warnings I had read about taking photos of indigenous peoples and how they equate it to having their soul robbed, I decided there was no harm in asking. Communicating via an eight-year-old interpreter (the girls didn't speak Spanish, only their tribal tongue) I suggested a rider-and-pillion shot which met with a firm rejection. There was no way either of them was slinging a leg over this frightening metal beast. Thirty minutes, four Chile-Alaska stickers and a handful of foreign coins later, and negotiations were cemented. They struck rigid poses in front of the bike.

Locals stared at me as I rode through small mountain settlements, generally malevolently I noted. On one steep descent, a gang of four youths ran onto the road behind me, yelling abuse and throwing stones. "Keep a cool head," I thought as I flicked the bike through sharp bends which gradually broadened as I descended through the valley and approached the relative safety of San Cristobal de la Casas.

Lying at over 2,000 metres, this colonial gem is misleading. Crammed with charming churches, artisans and street traders, it gives off an initial atmosphere of a laid-back tourist town. The large numbers of military and riot police clustered around the town, however, soon focus one's mind on the more recent past of this troubled area. As in other Latin American war zones, it was difficult to engage in conversation with young men without wondering what dark secrets they were hiding.

The street children of San Cristobal are considerably less camera-shy than their counterparts in the *campo* and were more than willing to climb aboard the bike and strike a pose in exchange for a few pesos. They clustered around me, a sea of brightly coloured little woolly hats, dirt-streaked faces and gap-toothed grins, hands outstretched for a 'posing fee'.

The Parador Mexicana, a pretty motel with an attractive ornamental courtyard, is a motorcyclist's dream. I could park my bike less than a metre from the pillow of my bed and sleep soundly, happy in the knowledge that there was an armed security guard at the gate, in the event of any Zapatista uprisings that night. I retired to bed after a satisfying steak at La Prillada, a fondue and parilla restaurant: what you might call Swiss-Argentinian fusion in a backdrop of cowboy artefacts and bar stools fashioned out of saddles.

The aforementioned zoo at Tuxtla proved to be a lot further than I thought. It's heralded as having the largest selection of indiginous Chiapas animals anywhere. I began to question the wisdom of riding for a day and a half to see any kind of animal, Chiapan or otherwise. Still, banking the bike over on tightly curved mountain roads was no hardship I thought, as I cruised into the lush province of Oaxaca, my pleasure marred only by the jolting speed bumps one hits when passing through any village in Southern Mexico. Even with paralever and telelever suspension and lots of suspension travel, these bumps can loosen your fillings at anything above a snail's pace. Some are marked, others not, making them potentially lethal at night.

The zoo was all it's cracked up to be, the animals kept in very

Indigenous girls, Tuxtla

large enclosures which reflect their natural habitats – so large that at times I had difficulty spotting them. A gang of teenage girls had no difficulty spotting me as a lesser-spotted leather-backed gringo. They queued up to sit on my bike and have their photo taken. One of them stroked my hair to see if gringo hair felt any different.

A fast blast along a dead-straight plains road brought me to the outskirts of Tehuantepec. Stopping at yet another military road-block, I asked the soldiers if they'd be prepared to pose with the bike. As I crouched down to create some interesting upshots, two giggling teenage Indian girls, who had previously been flirting with the soldiers, came up behind me, stroked my hair and recoiled in fits of giggles. Reading this, you're probably thinking "Wow! this guy must have weird hair!" But no, it's pretty average reddish-blonde issue. The barber I visited in Tehuantepec the following day certainly did not treat it with any great reverence, sending me out in under three minutes with a standard-issue crappy Indian haircut. I sought solace in a tamarind juice from a market stall, which sounded romantic but which tasted like pond water.

Tehuantepec does a very good Saturday morning market. Being

a very matriarchal society, the Zapetec Indian women run the majority of the stalls, having dragged their produce from the villages. They are tough saleswomen who take few prisoners. A couple of hours of this is more than the average punter can take, so I took a strange-looking three-wheeled rickshaw back to the Hotel Cali, where I was staying. The rickshaw had what can best be described as a chariot attached which one stood up in and gripped a horizontal bar for stability. I felt like Boadicea amidst the Iceni.

Tehuantepec is well known for the high quality hammocks that are produced there. I spent the entire afternoon lazing in one by the side of the Hotel Cali's pool. I soon lost interest in my paperback as the pool filled up with a group of extraordinarily beautiful girls. Chatting to them, I learnt they were "on a course". I assumed it must be exclusive to goddesses because that's just what they were. There was talk of meeting in the hotel disco later. I was in no doubt where I would be ... .

*   *   *   *

Mexican discos, I decided, were too loud, too dark and too full of men in white trousers on the pull – not that they ever seem to get anywhere. I decided to take an 'early bath' in anticipation of the 400 mile ride I would face the following day. Seasoned bikers reading this will no doubt think "400 miles? Huh...a doddle!". That may well be if you're riding down the M40, or some lavishly tarmacced Route National in France, but dodging goats and donkeys on Mexican mountain hairpins with a Pancho Villa lookalike bearing down on you in a knackered old cattle truck is quite a different matter.

En route to my room I bumped into my poolside lovelies, this time in slinky evening gowns with their hair pinned up, tendrils dangling sexily on their naked shoulders. I realised this was not a home job when two guys whose bleached crewcuts screamed 'Mexican hairdresser' took up the rear, followed by a man with an armful of cameras who needed no further introduction. I discovered that they were, in fact, combatants for the crown of Miss Oaxaca and tonight was the finals. One of the girls invited me back into the disco. I was sorely tempted, but the prospect of three hours sleep and a thick head persuaded me to do the sensible thing and gracefully decline. I lay in bed reflecting that I must be getting old. She was probably just feeling sorry for me, anyway ...

I felt queasy and irritable when I awoke. My mood was not helped by firstly having an argument with the manager over my bill, then seeing a dead donkey in the road having its eyeballs picked out by a pack of vultures. The upside of the morning was a nice, grippy mountain pass. The mountainside was carpeted in cacti which grows out of the almost vertical face horizontally, then, in a bid to find sunlight, bends at a right angle and thrusts itself towards the sky.

The village of Santiago Matatian, a nondescript little place that merely punctuates the highway, would normally be somewhere to thunder through, were it not for its claim to fame as the epicentre of the world for the distillation of *Mezcal*, the fiery liquor that comes from the agave plant. The road through Santiago Matatlan is a seemingly endless line of *Mezcal* distilleries, outlets and tasting houses. Sampling *Mezcal* before I had even eaten breakfast probably isn't the best way to start a day, but under the shade of a palm tree with a solicitous proprietor plying me with various blended varieties, that's what I did. Blended immediately after distillation with fruit juices it makes a lovely velvety drink.

Mezcal is regarded as the drink of the South, while its counterpart, the more universally known *Tequila*, comes from Jalisco in the North of Mexico.

A little further up the road I hit a DEA (Drug Enforcement Agency) roadblock manned by about half-a-dozen fresh-faced soldiers and their captain, who after asking me a few general questions as to my nationality, destination, purpose of trip, etc., casually enquired "So, how do you like to smoke cannabis?" When asked damn fool questions like this I'm tempted to respond, "Out of a clay pipe, actually, with a little Wagner playing in the background – how about you?" I can't imagine they expect anyone with half a brain cell to fall into their clumsy trap.

Oaxaca had all the makings of a great overnight stay. A big, happening city, crammed with splendid colonial architecture. My stomach felt extremely delicate. I thought lunch might help, but the sight of the big fish head floating in my *caldo de pescado* made me feel a lot worse. It was much too early to settle here and I had a lot of riding ahead of me. I knew I could make it a lot easier by breaking one of my unwritten rules. Did I want to take the regular road – about eight hours of speed bumps, roadblocks and hordes of VW Beetles – or would I do the unthinkable and take the hugely expensive autopista, which would take half the time? Despite not being in the 'spirit' of the journey I opted for the latter and hunkered down for a 110 mph blast through the Oaxaco valley. The two-lane highway was deserted, leading me to think if they dropped the price a little they might find some customers. I switched to the free road for the last 100 kilometres, passing through various dustbowl villages and sparse, arid flatlands, even-tually arriving in the city of Puebla de Zaragoza at 9.00 p.m..

The full pleasure of Puebla did not really hit me at first glimpse. Like a lot of Mexican cities, it's not particularly well-illuminated at night. The true charms of this Indian town can be fully appreciated in the morning while strolling around the *Zocalo*, a graceful square fringed with arcades, under which old men play chess and sip coffee, gazing appreciatively at the fine examples of womanhood parading up and down. I absorbed this scene through my zoom lens. I was on a mission to bring my 'women in uniform' series up to date. I had snapped a few attractive policewomen in various coun-tries and was eager to add Mexico to the list. This exercise involved darting behind a succession of lamp-posts in a bid to get the perfect candid shot. After tiring of this game, I loaded the bike and prepared myself for the most challenging of cities, Mexico City.

I could find no alternative to the autopista to get me to Mexico City. It was possibly the most expensive one I've ever travelled on. Mexico City has 20 million inhabitants, each of whom are issued with warnings from local authorities not to smoke, exercise outside or do pretty much anything outside, due to the appalling air qual-ity. With its endless shanty towns and propensity to earthquakes, I failed to see why anybody would willingly live there.

There is only one way to tackle one of the world's most congested thoroughfares like Mexico City's Periferico, and that's to attack it on a big kick-ass bike. The trick is to stay ahead at all times, filter aggressively and generally keep your wits about you. I did all these, made astonishing progress across this fearsome city and was soon on the road to Queretaro, a much more agreeable city. Lying at the foot of a string of 18th-century missions, Queretaro's first offer-ing to me was the Mirabel, a 70s-style business hotel. I felt I had to immerse myself in some culture to counteract the lack of soul in my hotel, so I parked the bike in the underground carpark, gave the *muchacho* a brief rundown on how to wash a BMW motorcycle and headed for the Plaza Obregon. The centre of Queretaro is pedestrianised, a rare thing in Latin America. I enjoyed *mole poblano* – chicken baked in chocolate sauce, chilli and grated coconut. It may sound awful, but it's surprisingly good and like manna from heaven after an endless diet of *tortillas* and *carne molida* (shredded beef). Plaza Obregon, like any Latin American square, is full of families wandering, listening to mariachi bands, meeting friends and so forth. What always amazes me is how incredibly late they keep their young children up. You could spend the entire night in a nightclub, stagger home bleary eyed in the early hours of the morning feeling like a true night owl, and there would still be five-year-olds on the street – easily outstripping you.

One would assume that the closer one gets the USA the cheaper it is to phone there. An incorrect assumption that resulted in a pre-departure debate with the Miramar's receptionist. I did think $50 was a bit steep to say "Hi, how are you?"

*   *   *   *

I was not getting any nice long stays anywhere in Mexico, so I resolved to do a two-day hard ride which would give me two full days of rest in Chihuahua, my next major mail and money pick-up.

I stopped at Aguas Calientes to browse around a funfair. Nothing conveys the atmosphere of Mexico better than a funfair, with its background of mariachi music, teenage girls flirting with the town's young bucks, endless tacky gift stalls and ageing rides that threaten to electrocute you at best or career off their rails at worst. I recalled a similar funfair in Ensenado, Baja California some years before: the smell of diesel, fried beans and two rides on the waltzers. I felt sick for a week. The funfair owner at Aguas Calientes was a kindly old man. He had all his young sons running around helping me to set up some atmospheric photos. I gave him one of my expedition stickers. He gave me a huge toothless grin and promptly put the sticker on his bicycle.

The road from Aguas Calientes to Durango via Zacatecas is a long, barren grind, saved only by the spectacular purple hue framing the mountains as the sun set on them. Durango is quite a contrast: cool, green and dotted with pleasant little parks and architecture that has a look of solidity and purpose. I rode into town very late and spent a lot of time finding the right hotel, in this case the Florida Plaza Motel.

I managed to find a sushi bar – a rare sight in Northern Mexico – which was still open. Good food, but the atmosphere of a morgue. They need a few Japanese salary men to brighten the place up.

Driven out of my room at the crack of dawn by neighbours playing music at ear-splitting volume, I set off on the 400-mile ride to Chihuahua, pausing only to let my inconsiderate neighbours know what I thought of them.

With the exception of Hidalgo del Parral, which lies roughly between the two cities, there is little but low mountains and arid prairie, save for the almost welcome respite of the occasional DEA roadblocks. This is one of the last opportunities the US government has of stemming the flow of drugs up north and the officials who clustered under a sun umbrella at these lonely outposts clearly knew what they were about. We had a jocular exchange at one roadblock. The leader of the group performed a camped-up impersonation of a 'typical Englishman' to the amusement of the others present, then quizzed me on everything down to the value of my jacket and jeans. I watched sniffer dogs root through the trailers of pickups and lorries.

Eating a beef sandwich in a cramped little diner in Higaldo del Parral, I noticed something unusual. In the deserted, baking hot midday streets of this 100,000 strong town, the only people to be seen were mariachi bands trudging around with their double basses and accordions under their arms, sombreroed to a man. Denied the luxury of the band favourite – a Transit van – they walked from gig to gig.

A bikewash was first on the agenda when I reached Chihuahua. I'd hit a swarm of locusts at speed. It felt like I was being pelted with shotgun pellets. The end result was an impressive roadkill which blanketed the front of my bike. A girl was standing waiting for her car – skin of alabaster, thick lustrous glossy hair. Was it Japanese I could see in her eyes? Yet she had the curves and height of a well-bred Spaniard. I had to speak to this beautiful, unusual girl. She introduced herself as Addis and explained that she was half-French and half-Japanese, but was born and bred in Chihuahua. I found out she was a radio and TV journalist. Would she like to meet me for dinner? No, she was going to work. Breakfast? She agreed to this and so the following morning I found myself in the restaurant of the Tierra Blanca Motel gazing at her beautiful face,

Mariachi band, Hidalgo del Parral, Mexico

marvelling at those jet-black lashes lowering seductively towards her fruit salad.

Sadly, Addis was moving to a new job in Mexico City that very afternoon. I appreciated the couple of hours she had spent with me on her very last day in Chihuahua.

This far north in Mexico it became clear that the menfolk liked to ape the 'Drugstore Cowboy' look: large white Stetsons, tooled belts and ornate cowboy boots made from the hide of some exotic reptile or other. There are enough shops in Chihuahua exclusively selling Stetsons and cowboy boots to service every would-be cowboy from Matamoros to Montana. Unsurprisingly, they were all empty.

Small towns with a mere handful of inhabitants boast ten bars, each one identical. Customers are expected to sit in a line at the bar nursing their Coronas before heading off to the Taqueria for a nocturnal snack. Fancy a little tapas with your Corona? Perhaps Thai would be nice tonight? Forget it. When Mexicans latch onto a product or service they bleed it to death. There is a staggering lack of marketing savvy or identifying the needs of the customer. Too many times my order had been taken in a restaurant by an untrained individual, promptly forgotten, then (if it arrived at all) all brought together – starter, main course, dessert and bill. They never forget the bill. I can't work out why they don't learn from their neighbours up north that service is important, and to consider

the customers' needs. Likewise, why don't more franchisers oper-
ate south of the border? Potential customers are thinly dispersed,
but overheads are very low also.

One bizarre example I saw of misguided marketing was someone in Oaxaca selling satellite dishes ... to people waiting at traffic
lights. "Yes, I'll have a stick of gum, a screen wash and give me one
of those satellite dishes" ... I don't think so.

The sun beat down viciously on a drab and deserted downtown.
Chihuahua had spilled outwards like North American cities leaving a forlorn and forgotten centre. There were very few people and
not a small hairless dog to be seen. In a bid to escape the blistering
sun I dived into a darkened bar, desperate for the cool caress of air
conditioning. I lined myself up on a barstool next to a long line of
Stetson-hatted men gazing vacantly into the blackness of the
cavernous room. Youths humped huge speakers around in readiness for an afternoon disco. The only girl in the bar, an Indian of
about 25, perched herself on the stool next to me and attempted to
converse. I thought my Spanish was failing me, until I realised it
was Indian symbols she was trying to draw on the back of my hand.
I got the gist from her unintelligible speech that she was a
Tarahumara Indian – great runners, who are fabled to be able to
outstrip a galloping horse. This one was not planning on doing any
running, just a hell of a lot of drinking. She had a very clever knack
of thrusting her cleavage in my face and putting yet another
margarita on my tab – all in one fluid movement. I walked out of the
bar a poorer but wiser man.

I felt sad the following morning. I had covered 13,400 miles
until this point, all on Latin American soil, and in five hours I
would be crossing the border into the USA. I love Latin America –
warts and all. I realised I would sorely miss it. Most people would
be enthusiastic about returning to a country where everything
worked, where low-level corruption was rarer, where all you had to
do in the event of a breakdown was to call a toll-free number. No
pollution, banditry, extreme poverty. Sanity. Yet I loved these
people ... Latins ... and knew at that point I'd be back soon.

My last breakfast at a roadside diner on the straight desert road
to Ciudad Juarez was the usual – *huevos rancheros*, plenty of *tortillas*. The waitress got the order wrong, but smiled like an angel in
apology. Adios Mexico

Chapter 20

"Hey! D'y'all speak English in England or what?"

Amerian stereotypes were out in force at the control office in Juarez where vehicle bonds are discharged. A young man from Kansas approached me, who at first glance seemed fairly normal: "Hey, guy, great bike! I'm in a boy band y'know – lead singer 'n all" (gives me rendition of forthcoming release). "Nice jeans, how much? Hey, d'y'all speak English in England or what?"

Racial stereotype number two was a minibus full of Friends of Jesus from Arkansas. A cleaner-cut looking group of people one could not find. Girls with blonde pigtails and braces on their teeth, earnest young men with goofy grins, sensible haircuts and razor-sharp creases in their chinos. The driver informed me that they were Christian missionaries. Basking in the glory of a major coup: "Last night we visited a small village of about 60 inhabitants near Chihuahua and you know what?" He gazed at me intently and paused for effect. "Twenty-five people let God into their lives last night. Yes, we saved twenty-five souls". I hadn't the heart to point out that Mexican villagers will probably invite just about anyone into their lives if you treat them right and give them a few freebies.

The local police were taking an inordinate interest in the medication of one of the young Christians. I interpreted for them and explained to the police they were merely travel sickness tablets. During the prolonged debate about the poor guy's motion sickness tablets I watched Mexicans drive past who were so villainous looking they probably frightened their own mothers. They passed unmolested ...

The border officials were kindly and undemanding. I even had to ask them to stamp my passport. From where I was standing it looked like anybody whose skin tone fell under the definition 'white' was given only the most cursory glance. This was, after all, prior to September 11th. The corpulent immigration official deduced I wasn't a wetback and drawled, "Welcome to the United States, Sir, y'all have a good trip".

The Comfort Inn on El Paso's Airport Drive leaves you in no doubt as to its religious leanings. Each room has the customary oversized bible and a Christian Directory. The latter is a substantial tome encouraging service seekers to patronise the businesses of other God-fearing folk. Rather than show photos of their vast used car lots, the likes of Dale and Lu-Anne prefer to be photographed with their kids and dog by their fireplace, imparting the right 'Christian message'. I remain unconvinced of the sincerity of it all. My fellow Comfort Inners were obese, loud and thoroughly obnoxious. I could not bring myself to lie by the pool for the sight of five-bellied 12-year-old children shovelling Doritos into their mouths.

On Sunday morning, after a lie-in spent skimming the evangelical phone-ins on TV, I rode three blocks down the street to a Harley Davidson dealership which billed itself as "largest in the world". They ran an all-day barbecue for customers each Sunday which could be enjoyed between treks around the vast showroom, accessories and clothing department. There cannot be many people left in the world who are unaware of that most powerful of brands: Harley Davidson.

I watched scores of middle aged men: lawyers, accountants, ZZ Top lookalikes, tattooed, untattooed, women, wannabees ... the lot, scooping up armfuls of Harley Davidson T-shirts, leather waistcoats, bandannas, coffee mugs ... the list goes on forever. I once owned a modified Harley Sportster but could never relate to the 'lifestyle' and gimmickry. I wandered around the parking lot, through the legions of folk purring appreciatively over each other's leather chaps until I came across Phil, the only person present who I felt sure had never contemplated the purchase of leather tasselled, factory endorsed underpants.

Phil is a proper biker. He rides a slightly ageing K-series BMW which he puts serious mileage on. He loves to ride and talk bikes and, if forced to choose between his bike and his children, might need a minute to think it over!

I met up with Phil that night at a grill-your-own-steak joint. It always interests me how man's hunter-gatherer instincts come out in these places. They just love to hold slabs of meat over naked flame – I would rather give somebody two bucks to do it for me. The bearded Phil (standard length, not ZZ Top variety) told me about the many countries he had worked in as a roving production manager for Wrangler Jeans: countries as diverse as Haiti and Southern Ireland. As a fluent Spanish speaker he had, of course, spent long periods working in Latin America.

*   *   *   *

There is no direct south-north state highway between El Paso, Texas and Albuquerque, New Mexico, so I was forced to use Interstate 25. The 260-mile trip, once past the glittering glass skyscrapers of downtown El Paso, now amounted to little more than desert. The small town of Truth and Consequences beckoned me from the Interstate. A green chilli stew, the signature dish of New Mexico seemed a good idea. As I sat in a little café full of blue-rinsed matrons, or 'seniors' as they are euphemistically called in the States, it was explained to me how 'Truth and Consequences' got its name.

This was a popular TV game show in the 1950s. As a publicity stunt the programme makers offered a large cash sum to any town that was willing to change its name. This sleepy desert town with little else going for it, other than a place to die, leapt at the opportunity. The neighbouring town of Elephant Butte probably felt it was already appropriately named, judging by the bulky forms of most of its residents.

The dip in evening temperature came as a welcome relief from the gruelling daytime desert heat. As I cruised into Albuquerque I knew there was just one place I had to be: Route 66 – the Mother Road. A living icon to the golden age of American road travel. Nowhere can Route 66 be seen in as much of its original glory as downtown Albuquerque. I gave the Old Town the once-over first. A very attractive couple of blocks of old Adobe-style buildings had been spoilt, in my opinion, by too many Native American gift shops. A tad contrived for my tastes. Route 66 was a different matter altogether. My scalp tingled with excitement as I drank in the faded glamour of America's Main Street: the diners, run-down motels and bars with their glitzy neon signs jutting out, transported me back to the 1950s. The more run-down motels offered monthly rates as a low-cost housing alternative to penniless drifters.

I checked into the promisingly-named 'Paradise Motel' before

heading off to an appealing bar-restaurant with a large patio that I
had spotted earlier.

Sitting nursing a cold wheat beer and absorbing the magic of
Route 66, I was approached by a man of my own age, who could
best be described as unconventional looking. Jim had a shaven
head, a long goatee beard that touched his chest and various bits of
facial jewellery. He was clutching a copy of Herman Goering's
diaries. He introduced himself and his girlfriend Mary, who was
waitressing – she was clearly a tough little cookie from Chicago, but
with a heart of gold. They treated me like an honoured guest, plying
me with beer as Jim told me of the fifteen-odd motorcycles he
owned, along with a small motorcycle repair business. Mary was a
keen biker too, having been heavily involved in the R and D of Buell
Motorcycles. BMWs were Jim's thing. He had spotted mine parked
up and was eager to elicit information.

As the table began to groan under the weight of the bar's
home-brewed beer, I made the decision to drop the bike off at the
motel before heading off with them for yet another green chilli stew
and a few games of pool in a dark cocktail lounge. We played
doubles with a plump, homely-looking girl and a stocky Native
American called Leon. "Hey, man, you're a mother-fuckin' gentleman and a scholar!" exclaimed an inebriated Leon, excited at his
first encounter with what he regarded as an English gentleman.
"And how's that mother fuckin' Queen of yours man?" I didn't take
offence at his unorthodox term of address for our monarch. I soon
learned that "mother fuckin'" was a word that Leon used like others
use personal pronouns. Jim and Mary dropped me off in the early
hours of the morning, drunk as a lord. I slept the sleep of the dead.

Needing to eat something distinctly European, as opposed to
green or red chilli stew, I awoke late and headed straight out for
lunch, in the hope that a full stomach might improve my hungover
state.

"Would Sir welcome a little shaved Parmesan?" enquired the
rather effete waiter in the elegant Northern Italian eatery. Large
overhead water tanks dispersed an ultra fine mist. Sufficient to
cool their pampered clientele without destroying the ladies' $35
blow-dries. There was not a chilli stew to be seen.

I found Jim in his workshop-cum-crashpad surrounded by
dismembered motorcycles. Not wishing to encourage the attention
of the authorities, Jim's customers had to practically phone ahead,

then give a password at the door. Never needing much of an excuse for a beer, we rode up to Kelly's Bar and spent the evening chatting to two of Jim's friends, a devastatingly pretty Mexican girl and a 4' 10" 'exotic' dancer, who talked matter-of-factly about her groin-thrusting activities in the world of Adult Entertainment.

Jim, Mary and I had planned a ride-out into the mountains the following day. Jim was feeling unwell so after a late breakfast (red chilli stew, unsurprisingly) we bade our farewells.

State Highway 44 to Farmington passes initially through barren terrain punctuated by the odd adobe building or Navaho Indian reservation. I was staggered by the proliferation of casinos on the reservations. In the early '90s I had been travelling around the tri-cities region shared by Illinois and Iowa and had witnessed the initial relaxation of the country's arcane gambling laws. Mississippi paddle steamers were the very first to be granted gaming licences. Native American reservations were next on the list, the Government believing, quite rightly, that these beleaguered people were overdue a break. Unfortunately, this overnight boost in the prosperity of the reservations has created as many social problems as it has cured. Alcohol-fuelled domestic violence and drug abuse have risen significantly.

It was with some relief that I started my ascent of the San Juan mountains. The desert heat of Texas and New Mexico had been so fierce that returning to the bike, I was sometimes unable to touch the brake and clutch levers, they were so hot.

Chapter 21

The Million Dollar Highway – Colorado

Durango, Colorado, nestles high in the San Juan's, a once flourishing mining town, it has now traded this in for the more lucrative tourist industry. Durango's tourist board knows just what the punters want – a sanitised Old West experience with a few adventure sports thrown in for the more athletic visitor. They achieve it admirably though can go a little far. "Howdy, pardner!" stated the parking warning I picked up on Main Street. It went on in floral Western lingo to list my misdemeanour in the nicest way possible and then to wish me a great day. I decided, on balance, that I probably preferred the "piss off!" variety, as issued in England.

Durango's 19th-century heritage is evident nowhere more than on Main Street. Traditional wooden buildings rub shoulders with majestic brick Victorian hotels. At regular intervals throughout the day a lovingly restored steam train bisects Main Street on its way up into the mountains, laden to the brim with excited tourists.

I dined in an overpriced steak restaurant surrounded by healthy, glowing, attractive young people exchanging tales of white-water derring-do and technically challenging rock climbing exploits. I felt slightly out of it.

The usual demands of laundry, rest, etc. kept me in Durango for longer than was necessary. The truth was I had extended the dates of my trip by ten days and was, for once, ahead of schedule.

I got chatting to a young guy of nineteen outside a gas station. Burt was riding a shabby Suzuki Katana 750. He clearly invested a greater percentage of his pocket money into his two-tone hair, wraparound shades and baggies than into his bike. He suggested that we go for a ride. I sensed that Burt's youthful arrogance would make this an opportunity for him to show off and introduce me to his perceived phenomenal riding skills. I played along with it.

Burt's hapless passenger was dumped in town, abandoned for improved manoeuvrability of the machine. We rode every mountain road that Durango had to offer. Burt desperately tried to burn me off. I stayed glued to his back wheel without the slightest effort. We stopped for a juice. I tried to gently suggest ways that Burt could improve his road progress and ride more safely at the same time. It fell on fairly deaf ears. Deciding he had little hope of impressing me as a motorcyclist, Burt resorted to image-enhancing claims like "Hey, man, because I trust you ..." (I'd known him for 45 minutes) "I'm going to let you into a very private secret." "What's that Burt?" I enquired with mild interest. "I'm a pothead, man!" he boasted proudly, looking at me with delirious eyes.

*   *   *

Tired of adolescent point scoring I headed into town for a couple of margaritas and the largest plateful of burritos, chimchangas and tamales that a human could possibly consume.

My Durango experience improved dramatically when I met Rachel, a pretty Native American girl working as a receptionist at my motel. Our first date was not a starred event. Our pleasant lunch was marred by being asked not to smoke, on the outdoor patio of all places. Not only was the patio completely devoid of people but so was much of the restaurant. Pondering over this example of smoking Nazism, I watched Rachel trying over and over again to crank over the motor of her ancient Ford truck. The truck was a family heirloom and, despite Rachel's obvious fondness for it, it did not merit much expenditure at the garage. A kind passer-by lent his support and over the course of the afternoon we traipsed backwards and forwards to Auto Zone – first to pick up a battery ... no success. A battery strap, solenoid and various bits of hardware followed, by which time I was beyond first name terms with the parts assistant at Auto Zone and was now looking at photos of his kids. Several hours later and after more trips to Auto Zone than I care to remember, the primeval beast rumbled into life and the lazy V8 burbled its way to Rachel's apartment.

We relaxed in Rachel's compact apartment watching a TV that showed only two channels clearly. I had watched the same advertising feature about 15 times and was practically poised to phone the toll-free order number and claim my Kwik-Mix food blender. A visit from Rachel's friend, Lisa, gingered up the entertainment on offer.

Lisa had had a love life dripping with Shakespearean drama. Her Welsh ex-boyfriend had managed to get himself full spouse rights due to some arcane technicality involving the co-signing of documents. The once-successful architect decided drawing up building plans gave too slow a return, so started taking credit card deposits for luxury cruises. Only one problem ... no ship. He swiftly moved to taking large deposits on 'prime' real estate where he was due to build some exclusive homes. He never had any intention of building anything. He now languishes in a Texan jail.

Boyfriend number three (she previously had another messy divorce) never took his sunglasses off, except maybe for bed. He never spent any of his own money, but did manage to get through $25,000 of Lisa's. Lisa felt that three years without sexual contact was a little under the national average for healthy couples. After hearing every excuse in the book from being simply tired to "I have to conserve my energy for tomorrow" (he didn't work), Lisa decided to confront the situation. She found out he was gay ...

Rachel and I went white water rafting on the Animas River. The water table was unusually low which did not exactly make for the thrill of a lifetime. As Rachel had become increasingly uncommunicative I decided that it was time to head out of town.

The Million Dollar Highway which would take me to Silverton had been built in the 1950s. Nobody seemed quite sure if the name was a reference to the construction costs or in reverence to the great views it offers. It certainly made me feel good as I swooped down its straights and keeled the BM practically on its side for some delicious hairpins.

There's only one way to truly appreciate the 'western experience' in its purest form and that is on the back of a horse, and so I found myself on a fine-looking champagne mare escorted by Marilee, a blonde pony-tailed, middle-aged woman with eyes as clear and blue as the open Colorado skies. We took a wide loop of narrow trails, passing copses of scented pines and a stunning aquamarine lake, which I tried to appraise in favour of the inviting view of Marilee's pert, denim-clad bottom jiggling six feet in front of me. At 10,000 feet the air was fresh, clean and a perfect temperature. I mentally listed it on my 'places to retire to', imagining myself barbecuing sirloin and gently rocking on the porch of my ranch with a Marilee-type at my side. I dismissed this ridiculous notion and mounted my steel horse for the ride down into the old silver-mining town of (not surprisingly) Silverton.

A town that sees more paper-hatted tourists than grizzled miners these days, Silverton – like Durango – has cleverly re-packaged its past. Tourists take the old steam train from Durango for a full-day 'western experience' culminating in a Main Street 'gunfight' which takes place every evening – a little wearing I imagine if you are there for a week. I entered a heavily adorned clapboard fronted café which boasted 'Funnel Cakes'.

"So you're from Germany? Well, you'll want apple pie. Y'all eat apple pie in Germany doncha?" The two middle-aged German tourists looked a little uncomfortable to be racially profiled in this way. They murmured assent. "An' doncha forget to put a pin in our map!" barked the waitress cheerfully, indicating a wall map that was a mass of coloured pinheads. From that moment they were referred to neither as Sir or Madam, but Germany, as in "Germany, d'ya want cream in your coffee?" I bolted down my pancake and fled, unwilling to be identified as a place name.

Gliding through pristine scenery, skirting the ski resort of Teluhride and slowing down for a sleepy little village, I suddenly became aware of a police 4 x 4 filling my rear view mirror, and the unmistakable wail of its siren. Without turning around I watched a corpulent figure drag himself out of the driver's seat, adjust his Stetson and amble towards me. I felt his mirrored Ray-Bans boring into the back of my skull. After carefully studying my documents he opened the corner of his mouth and drawled my 'offences', mainly doing a tyre-shredding 36 mph in a 25 mph limit and overtaking where there was a solid line. I politely pointed out (unwilling to encourage a $75 fine) that this practice was acceptable in Britain, as long as one did not physically cross the line – which I had not. "Well, that's England and this is Colorado, son." He eased the words out of the corner of his mouth. His lips barely moved. I sensed I was losing the argument. I was dealing with a man whose forefathers had been on physical terms with their cousins, and he was not about to become a bleeding-heart liberal. I played the innocent abroad to the hilt. It worked. He gave me a lecture and a warning ticket, which was not exactly of the "Howdy Pardner" variety, but beat a fine. He agreed that he did live in a county with absurd laws and that he did not necessarily agree with them but he had still have my ass if I committed another transgression of the law in the State of Colorado. He handed me his calling card – an animated picture of a pig in a policeman's uniform which he proudly announced was a self-portrait – and bade me farewell.

Chapter 22

On the Trail of
Donny Osmond

As Colorado merges into Utah so the landscape changes. Reddish rock formations punctuate a barren desert. Though not as impressive as Monument Valley on the other side of the State, Archer Canyon still makes a lasting impression as the sun sets on its towering edifices.

Despite upping the pace to a speed that would have every state trooper in Utah reaching for their notebooks, I still knew I would not make Salt Lake City by nightfall. There was only one other town of any size – Price, Utah.

I sat in a family diner-cum-Mexican restaurant, being subjected to Utah's clean air laws, meaning I couldn't smoke. One could probably drive out into the desert, 25 miles from the nearest habitation and have a sly ciggy, but somehow I doubt it. Utah's alcohol and tobacco laws are draconian at best. There's no doubting you're in a Mormon state. I read the public announcements taped behind the cashier's booth. These included the 'Castle Valley Pageant and Lamb Fry' or the equally earth-moving 'Open Youth Bread Baking Contest'. I decided this probably would not make my list of desirable retirement locations. I wandered into the subterranean bar that shared the diner and was relieved to find it was simply a matter of paying five dollars and one could become a lifetime member. Brandon, a likeable twenty-something involved me in his social circle "Hey dude! Come and meet some people!" he called out to me. And so I met Kathy, Peet, Texan Mike, Frank and Sylvia, a Navajo Indian. Friendly and eager to embrace me into their small blue-collar mining town we drank lots of beer and had a lot of fun. Nobody knew how dramatically their lives were about to change.

I arranged to meet Kathy the following morning. A bubbly blonde with a fun-to-be-with personality, we'd arranged the night before as it was to be her day off that she would show me the sights of Price. This would take all of fifteen minutes. I did not know what she had in mind for the rest of the day. She announced that she would have to nip back to her house for something, which was on a vast trailer park on the edge of town. I was perplexed and more than a little irritated when she didn't re-appear. I wandered down to the bar in the late afternoon in the chance that I might meet here there.

Kathy was there, with her friend Peet. Kathy's face was ashen, her eyes unfocussing. Peet's eyes were swollen red, she was mildly hysterical. I gradually drew it out of them ... the whole story. Peet's husband had decided to take a day off from his job working at the pit-face at the huge local coal mine. He had asked a young colleague to cover his shift, who, eager for the extra money, willingly agreed. Sadly, there won't be any more nights in the basement bar shooting pool with his buddies or trips to the Castle Valley Pageant and Lamb Fry. He was killed outright along with another colleague in a huge explosion at the coal face that morning. Eight other seriously injured miners had to be airlifted out.

A similar accident had occurred two years previously resulting in loss of life. This time the German parent company were taking no chances, they announced immediate closure of the mine, adding 350 workers to Price's already long list of unemployed. I felt desperately sorry for these decent, hard-working people. The future did not look good ... .

*   *   *   *

It's a strange town where the waitress in a restaurant brings you a beer and announces that she's not allowed by State Law to put it on the table until you've finished the dregs of the previous one. Welcome to Salt Lake City, Utah. I had been hoping for a relief from the oppressive regime of Price's restaurants. The previous night I had been forced to eat a revolting soup with the taste and consistency of rice pudding followed by a nausea-inducing creamy pasta dish in an environment that forbade alcohol consumption or smoking. I had hoped that things would look up in Salt Lake City, but I was not convinced. I decided that Donny Osmond and his brothers must have had a pretty crap youth.

I still felt unsettled by the events in Price. I had ridden past the deserted Willow Creek mine that morning. Union Pacific boxcars were hauling residual coal along the railroad, but the rest of the pit was ghostly quiet.

Although a modern city, famed for its cleanliness and safety, Salt Lake City has a smattering of historic buildings downtown. The Perry Hotel where I checked into proudly advertises its presence on the Salt Lake City's Historic Register. Temple Square at the very centre of Salt Lake City (S.L.C.) is the spiritual centre of the Mormon Church or, to give it its full title, the Church of Jesus Christ of Latter Day Saints (C.J.C.L.D.S.) . As President of the Mormon settlers, Brigham Young announced that this was 'the chosen place' which he had been led to by God. And so it evolved. Personally, my only contact with Mormons has been flicking through my cousins' Osmond Fanzines. Angela and Linda were devoted 'Donny girls' in the early 70s and even went as far as buying imported LPs of the illustrious brothers singing hymns. Their devotion knew no bounds. I've also seen briefcased and be-suited Mormon missionaries wandering around Macclesfield, attempting to 'blend in' – although the only way you would blend into Macclesfield would be to spend a day in a tattoo parlour beforehand. That's my lot really. I decided to take a trip to Temple Square and educate myself.

Over 50% of S.L.C's population is Mormon which probably explains why they don't stand out quite in the same way as they do in Macclesfield. The Desert News, S.L.C's daily newspaper called me in for an interview. Being Mormon owned, I fully expected to be interviewed by a stereotyped Mormon. In reality, it was no different to any other newspaper office. I walked the couple of blocks from the newspaper to Temple Square thinking I had let my imagination run a little wild and perhaps I was not in a town of pulpit-bashers after all.

Sister Shaffer sidled up to me, once I was safely ensconced within the boundaries of Temple Square. A devastatingly pretty Swiss girl, she kept the chat pretty general for the first five minutes before gently introducing the subject of God. I asked her first name, which she politely informed me she "wasn't able to reveal", heaven knows why. The C.J.C.L.D.S. knows just how to rope in suckers like me – bombard them with sweet, pretty, demure young girls. To counteract the obvious sexuality of their female missionaries, they clothe them in long-sleeved starched white blouses, long black skirts and sensible shoes. Unfortunately, it would take more than that to counteract lascivious thoughts in types like me.

The Temple Square soft-sell continued with the showing of a two-hour film chronicling the gruelling journey the early Mormon settlers made across America in their search for the 'promised land'. Having tackled a hostile reception at their previous temporary settlement in Illinois, the settlers undertook the long journey through the then lawless west before finally settling at the Salt Lake The film was no low-budget educational video, but a lavish, visually dazzling epic that would impress even the hardest heart. It had been given the full Hollywood treatment – romance, rivalry, despair ... all in a nice soft-focus package. Steven Spielberg would be proud to call it his own. The plush auditorium which bettered many a multiplex was quite an eye-opener for someone raised on frayed-collared vicars with sellotape on their spectacles, humbly passing around the offertory plate. This was slick!

After watching the hugely impressive Mormon Tabernacle Choir I walked away from a half-day of riveting entertainment, for which I had not paid a penny, and feeling good all over, which I suppose is Temple Square's intention.

Back at my hotel, chatting with the receptionist and with the Mormon's exceptional marketing skills still fresh in my mind, listened to the story of her childhood in Tupelo, Mississippi, the same small town which is known to millions as the birthplace of Elvis Presley – 'The King'. She told me that endless legions of fans visit the shotgun shack where Elvis was born, but there is a limit to how much time one can spend in a one-room shack, so within the hour they're all bussed out of town again, denying the folks of Tupelo their slice of the pie. I could not understand why a tour of Elvis's old haunts had not been organised ... where he played, where his Dad hunted, interviews with their barber, family friends, etc. The Mormons would have done it very differently ... .

Finding out that the Desert News feature was going to run at 11.00 a.m. that morning prevented me from hitting the road in the relative cool of the early morning. I took an early lunch at a smart brasserie opposite the newspaper offices, which, judging from the many photos on the walls of barely-clad men was run by gays. The food was the best I had tasted in Utah (not too difficult to improve upon). I hoped the conservative-minded Mormon folk of Salt Lake City could find it in themselves to forget their unease with alternative lifestyles, and visit this fine restaurant.

From top:

The Atacama Desert, Chile

With Cecilia Campos and the directors of Liga Chilena Contra Epilepsia

Schoolchildren in Caldera, Northern Chile

Opposite page, clockwise from top left: Machu Picchu, Peru; on the bike at Tamarindo, Costa Rica; Campesino in Honduras

This page, above: military checkpoint, Chiapas region in southern Mexico; below – life in the fast lane, Oaxaca, Mexico.

Views from Mexico: facing page – girl in traditional dress, Tuxtla Guttierez;
this page, from top – confident police officers and camera-shy girls, both seen
in Chiapas

Feeling lucky, punk? Royal Canadian Police motorcyclist, British Columbia.
Facing page: Washington State line

From top:
With my parents in Vancouver.

With Ted Simon in Cartagena.

Mission accomplished –
Anchorage, Alaska.

Chapter 23

Basque Separatists, Elvis Look-alikes and ... Carlisle United

Another State, another desert road – this time Idaho, whose claim to 'Famous Potatoes' embellished the licence plates of most vehicles that I passed. I streamed past an endless traffic jam of bumper-to-bumper chrome-clad monster trucks using the narrow gravel band that bordered the median. One petty-minded trucker decided he was not going to allow me past and closed my path. No problem, drop back two vehicles, find a small gap, blast past that knuckle-dragging cowboy on his other side and sit in front of him, turning my head to give him a wide grin.

Anti-social behaviour is not restricted to truck drivers in Idaho. In common with several other Western States, but more so, one notices a distinct shortage of races other than white, Anglo Saxons. Welcome to the home of the 'Aryan Brotherhood', who share the northern sector of the State with other white supremacist movements. The state of Idaho is understandably eager to hide this dark secret and you certainly won't see people wandering around in white hoods, but I found the thought somewhat depressing as I rode the open plains, past mile after mile of potato plantations on the road to Boise, Idaho's state capital.

A short, but violent storm had turned Idaho's big, bold sky into a violent clash of colours, a rainbow of such intensity I had never seen.

A trim, neat city, Boise, like many western cities has no great heritage to speak of; though certainly since my previous visit in the mid-nineties it had become more sophisticated. Bardenay, reputedly America's only bar-and-distillery was pointed out to me by the hotel porter where I was staying, as a place I might enjoy. And so I

Deep in the western plains of Idaho

found myself nursing a large Bloody Mary (home distilled of course) on a patio heaving with beautiful people, looking out on an unremarkable pedestrianised thoroughfare in this equally unremarkable town. A vast range of cocktails, baba ganoush and Moroccan chicken seemed more Islington than Idaho. It struck me that with the novelty of brew pubs waning a little, this could be next big thing. On a strictly illegal level it would be a great way of avoiding punitive taxes on spirits.

I watched a dedicated poseur cruise past the bar slowly (was it six or eight times?) on a new shiny Indian Chief replica, the rumble of the huge V-twin resonating through the traffic-free street. He predictably was not wearing a helmet. I had seen large groups of Harley riders that day, making the annual pilgrimage to Sturgis, South Dakota, home of the Black Hills Classic, which has now become an internationally famed orgy of all things Harley Davidson. Judging by their apparel, most of them were having a hard time deciding if they wanted to be Wild Bill Hickock or General Custer. Very few were wearing helmets, as indeed they're not required to in the Western States. Colorado had a law but it was repealed, no doubt on the grounds of the individual's 'rights'. Can someone explain the logic of this? I can pass a very basic motorcycle test in the State … of say … Utah. This will involve little more than riding around a few traffic cones at walking pace. I can immediately purchase a 200 mph superbike which I can ride (without helmet) to the local pawn shop, buy myself a nice Smith and Wesson .45 revolver, 'waste' a few innocent diners in the local McDonalds, before ploughing into an equally innocent pedestrian at a three-figure speed … .Yet, I cannot smoke within 25 feet of a public building or drink beer in excess of 3.2° proof, which I practically have to be vetted for in order to drink.

What lunacy. We in Britain should make the bike test cheaper and less complex but keep it tough, make us go on training courses, make us wear helmets … show the world that we produce the safest and most skilled motorcyclists. From what I had seen on the roads of Idaho, some of the 'Harley Charlies' wouldn't last five minutes on Britain's roads.

The leafy, pristine sidewalks that make up Boise's residential district, dominated by the mini St. Paul's Cathedral-style State Capitol building makes a pleasing stroll. A couple of hours of trudging around in baking heat looking for an American Express Poste Restante office did not put me in the best frame of mind. Less so, when the manager told me he had not been aware he was responsible for holding mail and had 'mislaid' it. Hot and frustrated, I sought the sanctuary of an elegant patio bar and let the ice-cold amber liquid soothe my parched throat. An intriguing, chic 42-year-old called Terri asked me what I was doing there, and so ensued a two-hour conversation. She told me her husband was on a menopausal motorcyclist's road trip. I would have liked the conversation to flow into dinner, captivated as I was by her beauty and gently flirtatious manner, but I thought it wise to stay on the 'right side of the tracks'. She told me all about Boise's large Basque population (Pyrenean dwellers as opposed to wearers of tight corsetry) and recommended a good Basque restaurant.

Capitol Boulevard proved to be the same street I had dined on the previous night, though this was the Basque Theme Park end, adjacent to the Basque Cultural Centre. The Elvis Costello look-alike waiter at 'Gernika' – 'Idaho's most authentic Basque dining experience' – told me of how the first Basque settlers had arrived in the early part of the 20th century (he could not be more specific than that) to seek work as sheep herders. Others followed later to escape Franco's one nation regime. Boise is home to the largest population of Basques outside their native territory. Although the authorities had done a pretty good job of giving Capitol Boulevard the 'Basque look', what it needed for greater authenticity, was the smell of bad drains and men urinating against walls.

'Elvis Costello' proved to be a fairly eccentric individual. He told me of his obsession with English league football. Fully expecting a role call of admired teams, like Manchester United, Arsenal and Chelsea, I was a little taken aback when he enquired "Tell me, how are Carlisle United doing at the moment?" I gently explained to 'Elvis' that Carlisle were basically crap and would most likely soon be spending their Saturday afternoons in towns like Nuneaton, Yeovil and Stalybridge. His eyes brightened behind the horn-rimmed spectacles at this prospect. Elvis was only interested in teams that were relegation prospects. It troubled me when he expressed an in interest in my home-town team of Bradford City.

*   *   *   *

Soft, arable countryside, studded with the occasional white-washed homestead gradually merged into pine forests and rolling hills as I crossed into the State of Oregon. Sparkling rivers and babbling brooks weaved alongside the road. I was following the Oregon Trail, so called after the trek, back in the mid-1800s, of a quarter of a million people, mainly farmers, who moved with their families in caravans of ox-pulled wagons from their homes in the mid-west to an unknown but hopefully brighter future in the new frontier. Though fraught with dangers and extreme climates, the pioneers got through by establishing a network of contacts with local Indians, who proved valuable trading partners, giving navigational help in return for goods.

As I rode up the main street of Pendleton, Oregon, I knew this was what I had been looking for all along – the very core of small-town western existence. A town with no pretence. Rusting boxcars abandoned by the railway track, not a gift shop in sight, plaid work shirts and Stetsons worn for practicality rather than as a personal style statement. I ate some home-made chilli chased down with an ice-cold Miller High Life in an old saloon, with beautiful Edwardian bar fittings and engraved mirrors. People came up to me, introduced themselves, shook my hand and welcomed me to Pendleton – great! Old ladies, teased and blue rinsed, local traders, ranch hands, pregnant mothers, the Sheriff's Department ... they were all there. Decent people and not a phoney amongst them. This was the backbone of America, this town. If only America could lose its sleazy politicians and cynical attitudes and become one huge Pendleton, it would never look back.

The Asian proprietor of my sleepy little motel gave me a true folksy western welcome. Coming from Bradford I'm used to Asian people with regional Yorkshire accents, but a full-blown western drawl comes as a surprise. I fully expected the spitting baccy routine.

Pendleton does have one tourist attraction which is mercifully hidden from view. It's the extensive network of underground tunnels and rooms that run under the centre of the town. I followed a small tour group down a sidewalk trapdoor into a dark labyrinth of tunnels. Dank and oppressive, they were built at the turn of the century, ostensibly as a place where businesses could store their goods, safe from theft in those lawless times. Chinese labourers who were building the railroad lived down there to escape racial victimisation. They also came in very hand as 'speakeasies' during prohibition. The tour was concluded with a visit to an above ground ex-bordello. We were told how the long-standing Madame, a well-respected local figure who adopted the role of welfare provider to her girls, making sure that all their educational and spiritual needs were met. She was quite munificent in her generosity, allowing the girls to keep 80% of their 'take'.

Apologising profusely for checking out two hours late, my little Asian friend merely beamed. "Hey, no problem pardner – y'all have a good trip!"

And so I pressed on – through miles of picture postcard pastures and hamlets.

*   *   *   *

A diner called Gasoline Alley in the small town of Dayton attracted me. I had just crossed into Washington, the last of the Lower 48 States and was ready for something cold and the sound of clinking ice, not to mention air-conditioned sanctuary from the merciless sun. As I studied the hot-rod themed decor with its posters of Hemi Cudas, tri-power Chevys and other glorious automotive icons from the 60s, a trio of bored-looking youths started chatting with me: "Where d'ya ride from man?" "Oh ... Tierra del Fuego, actually." "Where's that? Is that in California or sometin'?" "Southern Argentina, actually." "Cool." End of conversation. Somewhat worrying that these eloquent individuals would be the future custodians of the English language.

I'd phoned around a few BMW dealers trying to organise a service and a new set of tyres. Unfortunately, the only dealer who was able to do it at this short notice was in Post Falls, Idaho, meaning a 150-mile detour east into Northern Idaho, via Spokane.

After spending over an hour riding around Post Falls in search of a huge multi-franchise dealer that seemed to have disappeared into thin air, I came across Beaudry Motorsports tucked away in a remote industrial park.

Once located, I rode to the Coeur de Laine Lake and booked into the Cavannah Motor Inn which sits on its banks. Enjoying a thick cut of prime rib-eye beef while watching the lights twinkling on the lake, I made my plans for the following day. It would be a long one – half a day to complete the work, followed by a seven-hour ride to Seattle, where I was due to meet up with my parents the following day. They were flying out to meet up with me for a few days. I was bursting to see them.

Steve Beaudry, proprietor of Beaudry Motorsports, despite

With Steve Beaudry, president of Beaudry
Motorsports, Post Falls, Idaho

having the responsibility of a vast dealership stocking the ranges of thirteen different manufacturers, still found time to roll out the red carpet treatment. He sent me off with a 20% discount on parts and a free T-shirt ... in exchange for a couple of photos which he could use in the local press.

Heading west out of Spokane took me through about fifty miles of sparsely populated farmland. In places it followed the railway line where old, defunct boxcars lay ... Burlington, Union Pacific ... names synonymous with an untamed country. For me, the American railroad is the most romantic in the world.

Farmland gave way to a very different terrain – vast areas of sagebrush and scattered rock formations. The sun was setting over the rocks, giving them a deep orange glow – quite beautiful.

Onto the Cascade Loop, a nice, twisting stretch linking the small towns in the Cascade Mountain range. Arriving in the town of Leavenworth, I decided to make this my base for the night and leave the other 125 miles to Seattle till the morning.

The first hotel I came across at the entrance to Leavenworth looked appealing – an alpine-style inn on the banks of the river. I waited in the small reception area while the receptionist dealt with a customer on the phone: "Sir, are you aware of our policy that any cancelled room which would have to be paid for in full at the time of booking, cannot be refunded but may be exchanged for another room of the same value within 12 months? Oh yes, pets are charged at $100 a night ... " Do they get their own fluffy bathrobes at that price? The hotel owners, Doris and Hubert, had placed a list of "Do's and Don'ts at the Bayern-On-The-River". I was beginning to wonder if I had stepped back into one of Adolf Hitler's summer resorts.

I rode into town to sink a beer and escape this oppressive regime. A million fairy lights greeted me, threaded through the eaves of Bavarian and Tyrolean style buildings. This was not the Cascades, it was the Alps! Even the ubiquitous McDonald's was built in authentic Tyrolean style, in observance of the town council's strict ordinance. I found this out later while chatting to the barman at a Bavarian-style brew pub. I told him how all the fairy lights and ersatz Bavarian architecture reminded me of Solvang in California, the famous mock-Danish village. "That's exactly where the local council got their idea from," he replied. "Leavenworth was in a real financial mess in the 60s and they had to find a way of

bringing tourist dollars in. They saw Solvang doing it and thought –
hey, that could be us." There certainly seemed a very high propor-
tion of hotels to visitors. Perhaps they needed to adopt Hubert and
Doris's style of canine and feline extortion.

*   *   *   *

Sweeping through the scented pines of the Cascades enjoying
the crystalline morning air was heaven itself – the
bumper-to-bumper chaos of Seattle in strong contrast. Seattle
always had an image as being a relaxed, informal city. The
arrival of Bill Gates and other dotcom billionaires seems to
have changed the ambience of the city to one of naked ambition. The town had the smell of greed; I wasn't sure that I liked
it.

Nowhere on my entire trip had I experienced such difficulty in
finding a hotel room. I visited over a dozen hotels in all corners of
the city ... nothing. I was offered one or two shared rooms, but the
thought of three nights of my Dad's snoring put paid to that idea.

After a joyous reunion at the airport, I followed my parents
downtown on the bike, Dad gingerly nosing their rental car into the
stream of rush-hour traffic on Interstate 5. I'd eventually secured
the Comfort Suites, but on the basis that we may be subject to a
room re-allocation each night – such was demand for accommodation. An exorbitant price was charged – it looked like not only
might I be 'Sleepless in Seattle' but destitute too.

After a trip up to '0' level of the Seattle space needle for a stunning 360° panorama of the city, we headed for Pike Market, in my
opinion Seattle's greatest attraction – a fantastic farmers' market,
bursting with exotic produce and wonderful flower stands. Small
in-state producers displayed mind-boggling selections of preserves
based on dozens of different types of berries. In view of such munificent exotic produce, lunch in a Bolivian restaurant seemed appropriate. I was sorely missing South America and thought some
humanitas (maize pies with melted cheese) might bring it back.
Dad, never a huge lover of Third World cuisine, clearly thought the
same – in the literal sense – judging by his protestations.

There was an exhibition of Modern American Artists at the Seattle Metropolitan Art Museum which we'd been invited to by the
Gallery's administrator, Laura, a new-found friend whom we'd met
in a downtown bar. It seems the Gallery has conveniently forgotten

that David Hockney is, in fact, a Bradford lad and about as American as the Queen.

The Jimi Hendrix Museum held great fascination for me, having been a long time admirer of this local-boy-made-good. I learned that there had recently been a large dispute between the late musician's family and the owners of the Museum, resulting in a lot of choice exhibits being pulled ... shame. We went for lunch instead to a big untidy Italian restaurant, owned by a voluble Anthony Quinn type character. The food was excellent, non-homogenized, rural Italian cuisine. Our Anthony Quinn Nemesis came to the table to chat and smoke with us. It was delightfully non-Seattle.

I noticed a lot of disabled people in Seattle. I was told they favour the place because of the excellent facilities and wheelchair access available: they are certainly not there for the low cost of living.

It's a three-hour ride to the Canadian border. I'm sure it could have been a lot quicker but I had to tail a 30 mph rental car piloted by Michael Rhodes, who isn't a man who can be rushed. In fairness, I had delayed our departure from Seattle by three hours. I was penalised for this by a day full of my Dad throwing long sighs and clicking his tongue impatiently. Ahh ... the joys of family life.

"Now Dad, what I'd like you to do here is park up, follow that narrow trail by the campsite down to the river and we're going to get some good action photos of me fording the river on the bike. OK?" This did not go quite as planned, the large pebbles of the river bed slithered around under the bike's wheels. Unable to get a good head of steam in the short distance from the edge of the steep bank to where the water started, I sank like the proverbial stone, requiring Dad and a family of campers to drag me out. The ignominy of this was compounded when the camp warden came over to quote some State ordinance, forbidding motor vehicles from being driven in Washington's rivers. Strangely, my father never clicked his tongue once ...

Chapter 24

Beautiful British Columbia – Strange Inhabitants

Vancouver struck me as an odd city. I approached it through some down-at-heel inner city neighbourhoods, mainly populated by working-class Hong Kong Chinese, past a beautiful harbour gleaming with expensive fibreglass hulls and through a Hari Krishna procession. Eventually I arrived at the smart, elegant hotel we had pre-booked ... except it wasn't. Hotels of the Coast Plaza's standard normally have a lobby full of interesting-looking and glamorous people, not people in cycling gear that look like the fallout from a biological experiment that's gone wrong. I waited in the forecourt for my parents to turn up. Various guests stopped to quiz me about my bike. They were all very pleasant, but a bit ... well ... dim. I couldn't work the place out.

Vancouver is truly cosmopolitan. No one race seems to 'belong' any more than another. There's an almost tangible atmosphere of goodwill and tolerance.

I rented a mountain bike for the day and took off, cruising the boardwalk, sipping cappuccinos, getting burned to a crisp, though leaving a perfect outline where my Ray-Bans had been, in a fair bid to look as goofy as my fellow Coast Plaza guests. Deddy, a twenty-something rollerblader, had a coffee with me on the board-walk and gave me the low-down on Vancouver. She told me the city's current malaise was the brain-drain down to the States, where salaries are higher and the cost of living is lower.

I witnessed another exodus that evening, while dining in the Martini Bar. The place gradually emptied, diners flocking out to huddle on a tiny outside balcony. Was it the view perhaps? No, they were going out for a quick puff. The bartender explained that when Vancouver announced its clean-air laws, bars lost a large chunk of their customers practically overnight.

We reluctantly checked out of our cavernous suites at the Coast Plaza and had a final lunch together at a fashionable harbour restaurant, joined by Mark and Jane, an ex-pat daughter of one of my mother's friends. After a fond farewell, I started the long final leg of my journey to Alaska, way up in the frigid north. I had contemplated staying an extra day to attend some proposed press interviews organised by Rick O'Brien, chief executive of the British Colombia Epilepsy Society. There was no guarantee they'd be completed that day though, and the open road pulled me like a magnet.

Tranquil lakes, dense pine forests and a road that felt as though it was taking me into the great unknown, were my early experiences of the vast wilderness of Beautiful British Columbia. The great road snaked its way north, to the famous ski resort of Whistler. I had decided that my overnight stop was going to be much further on – the town of Lilloet, about five hours north of Vancouver.

Lilloet is a pleasingly modest little town. This is a logging town, relying heavily on the railroad that lies on the floor of the deep valley that forms its focal point. The trailer-park style motel where I stayed was set high in the valley giving fabulous views of the microscopic train steaming past.

Dina's is a popular little Greek café and was recommended as the only place worth eating in. It was full of vacationing French Canadians, a group of whom went out to look at my bike. Two of them examining the paralever front suspension in minute details could be heard muttering *'formidable!'* and were nodding enthusiastically.

It felt substantially cooler at night up in Lilloet. I was clearly going to be back into my silk thermal Long Johns soon. I looked at the vast area of latitude between Lilloet and Anchorage on my map and thanked God I would not be arriving there too late in the year.

After checking out of the Retasket Springs Motel I stopped at a gas station-cum-country store for some coffee and donuts. Two Honda Gold Wing riders whom I had met just north of Vancouver simultaneously rolled onto the forecourt, their two-wheeled Winnebagos pulling matching trailers laden with camping gear. I failed to see why they needed all that gear when their homes were in Vancouver and they'd be back there in a couple of days. My worldly belongings for a four-month, 19,000-mile trip took up a fraction of the space. One of the riders, a middle-aged native Canadian, did all the talking, explaining that occasional male bonding and communing with nature were pivotal to a successful marriage. I can only imagine he must have had an extremely crap marriage to want to share a tent with someone like his buddy, Ali, for a few days. Ali was from Iraq and specialised in asking dumb questions, like "Do they have maps in South America?" I was tempted to reply "No, but most filling stations do a good line in sextants," but bit my tongue. Ali would have missed the irony anyway.

I left the paved road at the small Indian reservation of Pavilion and took a gravel logging route, kicking up huge plumes of dust in my wake as I tried to rear-wheel steer around some of the sharper narrower bends on the mountainside.

I sat and watched my reflection in a crystal-clear lake, counting the tiny pebbles on its bed. Lack of environmental control in Latin America made drinking directly from lakes a no-no, however far from civilisation. This, on the other hand, looked ready to bottle.

Back on the tarmac at Clinton, I maintained a steady 95 mph, keen to cover some distance.

After fish and chips in a dark lounge bar at the uninspiring cluster of buildings known as '100 Mile House', I hunkered down over the vast fuel tank of the BMW for a long stretch of nothing but pine trees. Two hours later, I pulled in for gas at an isolated gas station-cum-everything. It had closed down permanently some weeks before, so said a notice pinned to the weather-beaten door. The faded wooden sign outside stated 'The Oasis'. It did not fill me with much hope of finding more fuel for some distance and I was low ... very low.

I enquired at the small general store – the only other building nearby – as to where I might find fuel. Barry, the proprietor, very kindly offered to drive me to his home, a few miles up the road where he had a couple of emergency jerrycans in his garage. We piled into his flat-bed pickup with four semi-tamed Arctic wolves, and set off. A strong, handsome man in his mid-forties, Barry had sadly been struck down by polio, giving him a hunched posture and forcing him to walk in a peculiar crab fashion. He told me wistfully that his days of bar-room brawls and womanising were now over, due to his medical condition. He lived alone in a ramshackle hut, deep in the woods. He expressed no self-pity and seemed resigned to his lonely existence. I felt sad for him.

*   *   *   *

Quesnel, the next major stop on Highway 97, is unremarkable physically, but does have a very incongruous-looking population. The large number of turbaned folk I saw on the streets looked to be Afghans. For the life of me I can not imagine what brought them to this remote, unforgiving place. I had seen a smattering of Chinese along Highways 99 and 97, predictably running small general stores and garages, but this was quite bizarre.

At the end of a long 100-mph blast, I pulled into the much larger railroad-service town of Prince George. This was the last major town before 250 miles of wilderness. A dull town of drab colours, not helped by the perpetually washed-out grey of the northern sky. Prince George had been visited by Prince Charles and Princess Diana as part of their Canadian tour. Of course, the usual media pack had followed them here. In their subsequent news articles, some British journalists had described Prince George as "a dull, grey town full of lumberjacks". When the good people of Prince George heard this they were not best pleased. The Royal couple, it has to be said, did not find anything in Prince George to fan the embers of their dying relationship. They divorced shortly after their visit. He should have taken her to 'The Keg'. I had a great steak there. Nice and cheap too, by Kensington standards.

My bike had developed a strange whistling noise which did not seem to be influenced by forward movement or increased revs. I drew to the conclusion that the fuel pump may have drawn in air due to the couple of occasions when I had run out of fuel. I hoped it wouldn't deteriorate. There was not a BMW dealership until Anchorage – still 1,850 miles away. My Sigma 200m lens for my camera had broken too to make matters worse, necessitating a costly replacement. The upside was that the manager in the camera shop did give me a very useful talk about the dangers of bear attack while out on the road.

It wasn't just the bears I needed to look out for either, according to a little bearded man I met in a gas station. He had ridden up with his friend from Arizona on a pair of 'bitza' trail bikes – bits of this and bits of that. He was riding home alone after his buddy had hit a deer at speed and had been forced to abort his trip due to the resultant broken collarbone.

I felt listless and unwilling to ride that day. I had spoken to other

riders about the depression that one can experience towards the
end of a long journey as the dream nears its end. I was determined
not to just go through the mechanical motions, but to wring every
ounce of pleasure from my odyssey.

North along a die-straight, pine-fringed highway, watching the
tumblers of the odometer rotate; there was little other entertainment on this monotonous road. The sky was washed a frigid pale
grey. Again, no gas stations. Was I going to make it as far as
Chetwynd? I knew I would not. I kept revs at a steady 3,000 and
avoided any acceleration or braking to eke every last drop of fuel
out of the depleted tank. I finally ground to a halt five kilometres
short of Chetwynd. There was nothing and nobody around.
Pushing a 250 kilogram motorcycle laden with gear is only an
option when it's a matter of life and death. The unwieldy size and
weight makes every few metres a struggle, but this is what I
attempted to do. I spotted a Mountie sitting in his police cruiser,
parked up in a lay-by. I tapped on his window and pleaded for a
ride into town. He gave me a cursory look up and down and replied
in a detached manner that he was unable to help. I cursed. The
Mounties might always get their man but they'll do sod-all to help
stranded motorcyclists.

Sweating profusely, despite the cold, I kept pushing until I
reached a small RV park which appeared to be in the sole custody
of a 12-year-old boy. He was unwilling to face the wrath of his boss
when he returned – a certainty if he allowed me access to the campsite's limited fuel stash. I eventually managed to get him to sell just
half a gallon to me – enough to get me to a gas station ... hopefully!

I booked into Chetwynd's Country Squire Motor Inn, bagging
the last available room. As I approached the remote north – God
knows, this was remote enough – I noticed motel prices climb and
availability decrease. Accommodation was at a premium. After a
Wiener schnitzel in an ersatz Swiss inn, I nursed a beer for a while
in Murray's Pub and studied Chetwynd's locals going about their
courtship rituals.

I got a good early start. It had taken me almost four months for
the penny to drop that if I cleaned my kit the night before there
would be fewer delays the following morning.

The first 60 miles to Hudson's Hope were accomplished easily,
until a dense freezing fog fell, chilling me to the bone. I could
barely see beyond my visor. I had seen the odd dead deer lying on

the road and was anxious that it wouldn't be me taking out the next one.

I eventually merged with the world-famous Alaska Highway at the small settlement of Wonowon. The Alcan, as it's known, would be my home for the next week.

Chapter 25

The Call of the Wild

Dawson Creek to Fort Nelson is an endless 350-mile corridor of fir trees. My mind would wander into all areas of abstract thought but the main thing that dragged me on was "what would the next town be like?" I built images in my mind of bawdy saloons, salmon bakes, elk steaks ... the pioneer spirit. That is, until I reached Fort Nelson. I limped the last few miles into town, desperately trying to conserve the dribble of fuel I had left.

Fort Nelson is a miserable little town, built around a gas processing plant. Aware that the next settlement was 200 miles away and would most likely be no better, I made a considered decision to stay there. It was Friday – I wanted a few beers and a bit of action. Hopefully, something nice to look at, other than bloody fir trees! I parked up and walked into what was considered to be the best hotel in town, to be confronted with two bored teenage girls at reception – tattooed, bejewelled faces, chewing gum. They brought new meaning to the term 'common'.

"May I have a room please?"

"Eighty dollars. Pay now."

"Is there somewhere safe to leave my bike?"

"Out back."

"But that's a piece of wasteland with no lighting, protection or windows overlooking i.t"

Girl shrugs and turns her back on me.

"Can't I park it on the boardwalk, tight against the wall so it won't cause an obstruction."

"No."

"Why not?"

"I don't make the rules Mister."

"Can I see the Manager please?"

Bawls into a backroom: "He wants to see you!"

A very overweight woman appears. She may have been a female wrestler – I was not sure. She actually sneered at me. I turned my back and walked out. If it was 1,000 miles to the next town, I would ride it. I certainly was not staying in this dump. Sadly, this was to be a familiar scenario on the Alcan. Tourists are regarded as a captive audience, and all too often treated with casual dismissiveness by the hotels, restaurants and gas stations that exist on their patronage.

Lakes and mountains abounded beyond Fort Nelson. Distant snow-capped peaks stood forbidding under an eerie gunmetal sky. The grandeur made me feel like I had arrived in Alaska, the final frontier, yet still I was in British Columbia.

I pulled into a lay-by to admire a stunning view. A plump, middle-aged woman was standing by her ageing Japanese compact, doing much the same. She had a look that Americans euphemistically refer to as 'homely'. We started chatting about the view and gradually her intriguing story came out. Melanie was a happy, bouncy woman, inclined to view her cup as half-full, rather than half-empty, but life with a drug addict and waster of a husband eventually reached crisis point. She had taken him back after countless affairs and drunken, maudlin confessions and promises to 'change his life'. It happened once too often and at 44 she knew it was her last chance. She walked out one night with her few modest possessions and packed them into her only real asset, her car. She was driving the couple of thousand miles from her home in Fairbanks, Alaska to Seattle, where she dreamed of starting a new life on her own. She had no friends, family or even contacts in Seattle, and very little money to support herself. She was saving what little cash she had by sleeping in her car. All she had was an iron will and a belief there must be something better for her out there. I was humbled by her courage.

After a productive 530-mile day I pulled into the Liard River Lodge, an isolated settlement containing a lodge, restaurant, RV hookup, two gas pumps and, judging from warnings I had received, more that its fair share of bears. The owner of the Lodge reinforced this, explaining what to do if I encountered a bear on the trail to the nearby thermal springs. The upper springs had been temporarily closed as they had become a bears' feeding ground. It was OK to visit the lower springs, as long as I "made a lot of noise, didn't carry food and pretended to be dead if confronted by one." She went on to tell me that "folks has been gittin' a bit jittery of late". This was in the recent bear attack on a family of four. The bear in question was a 'dump bear', using the local dump as its food source. The local authorities had closed the dump leaving the bear without a food supply. It had not honed its natural survival skills, such was its dependence on the scraps of humans. Half-starved and deranged it mauled the family, killing them all.

Armed with this comforting thought (and my Swiss army knife) I picked my way through the overgrown trail at 7.00 a.m. the following morning.

As I lay naked in the steaming sulphur springs, pointedly ignoring the 'Strictly No Nude Bathing' sign I thought to myself what do I do now if a bear decides to enjoy this wonderful natural phenomenon too, and I'm lying here stark bollock-naked? Float like a dead person and hope he's not in the mood for dead meat that day.

As I loaded the bike I watched the clouds grow angrier-looking by the minute. It would be a thoroughly miserable eight-hour ride to Whitehorse, capital of the Yukon, if the heavens were to open. I would take a short ride – two-and-a-half hours would get me to the small town of Watson Lake.

Dodging rainstorms, I met Don, a Kawasaki KLR650 rider, working his way south to Las Vegas via Nevada, on what looked like a dangerously overloaded bike, though he assured me it handled 'just fine'.

At that moment, a heavily kitted BMW R1150 GS rolled onto the dirt forecourt. Darrel, a middle-aged Florida businessman, had decided to drag himself away from the riveting world of 'manufacturing, decorative grooving and remodelling systems for existing concrete', and 'find himself' in Alaska. Maybe that's what we were all doing – a bunch of middle-aged men trying to make sense of their lives. Motorcycles must be getting a lot more reliable these days – not one of us had suffered serious mechanical problems.

Small herds of bison grazed by the side of the Alaska Highway, sometimes roaming in the middle of the road. I often came face to face with heavily antlered caribou, which would be in the middle of the road and hold my gaze until one of us made a move. Apart from these fascinating beasts, the most frequent sight on the Alcan was proving to be the R.V. These huge 'recreational vehicles' are the land-based alternative to yachts for those ready to retire, sell up and travel the world (well, the USA and Canada at least). The active

Motor-home (RV) drifter in her 'colours'

oldsters whom I met had often sold their principal homes to spend their twilight years aboard these gadget-filled luxury road liners. Motorcycle and bicycle adventurers were becoming more frequent sights too. Wherever you come from, Alaska is seen as one of the furthest corners of the world, and if you're doing it by road, that road will be the Alaska Highway.

Watson Lake on a wet afternoon is about as appealing as a bowel complaint. After a five-minute familiarisation tour I checked into the Watson Lake Hotel. Channel flicking in my 'cabin' (more like a B&Q garden shed), I found out from the local news channel that Watson Lake was in the midst of its Discovery Days Pageant, celebrating the town's gold rush heritage. I rode down to the local park to watch some locals dressed Klondike style, riding aboard amateurishly decorated floats. The uniformed Mounties policing the event looked the best candidates to win the fancy dress parade. I parked an attractive female Mountie aboard my bike for a 'woman in uniform' photo. The three male Mounties present did not look like men who liked to dress in ladies' clothing, contrary to the Monty Python lumberjack song, but who knows …

Watson Lake has one attraction, and it is a big one: Signpost Forest. Back in 1942 a homeside GI, working on the Alaska Highway, decided to erect a sign, pointing the way and showing the mileage to his home town in Illinois. He could have had no idea what he had started. Now there are about 10,000 such signs planted by people from all corners of the world. Each one proudly displays the visitor's home town.

Zoe, a six-foot redhead, stands a good head and shoulders above the mainly First Nation People (as they like to be known) of Watson

Lake. I found her working a summer job in a hardware-cum-fancy goods store. "Hey, do you mind if I write to you?" she enquired. "You can do more than that – you can have dinner with me tonight," I replied.

Over baked salmon in the Watson Lake Hotel, she told me that she hailed from Vancouver Island, BC and had an uncle up here in the Yukon. She's the kind of girl who gets pleasure from very small things, so did not find the prospect of a season in Watson Lake off-putting. I could handle about two days of the place – maximum.

She told me being attractive, fairly sophisticated and in a small female minority that she had received about three marriage proposals during her first week in Watson lake. After dinner she piled her belongings onto the night bus to Whitehorse. It would be a four-and-a-half hour ride for her to the Yukon capital, but served as a change of scenery for a few days, before flying back to Vancouver Island to finish her university degree. Fortunately, Whitehorse was my next destination too. We made plans to meet up.

*   *   *   *

I rode to Whitehorse on a freezing, wet afternoon, partly wishing that I could have gone on the bus. My fingers were numb and my boots were leaking. A slush-coloured sky showed no promise of any warmth ... ever.

I dragged my wretched form into Mukluk Annie's in the tiny hamlet of Atlin for a traditional Alaskan Salmon Bake – thick steaks of lake-fresh sockeye salmon grilled over mesquite chips – sensational. For anybody who has only ever eaten farmed salmon, it's the difference between a filet mignon and a fairground burger. Mukluk Annie's advertised themselves as "Run by Christians to Christian Values". I took this to mean they were not going to rip me off like the previous twenty joints on the Alcan.

Whitehorse is a pretty modest capital for a province as vast as the Yukon. I rode past the *S.S. Klondike*, a large permanently moored white paddle steamer, which forms a kind of gateway attraction to the town. It's the first and last attraction you'll see in Whitehorse.

Whitehorse plays heavily on its Klondike heritage. I met up with Zoe for breakfast and after a mini-tram ride we visited the intriguing museum where one can pan for gold, see old film archive of dancing girls and wonder at re-creations of early mining conditions.

Zoe and I wandered over to the *S.S. Klondike*. I rode, she tottered in her four-and-a-half inch heels. She obviously wasn't satisfied with being the tallest girl in the Yukon, and was challenging for the title of tallest girl in the universe.

I'd met a couple of Honda Africa Twin riders in Whitehorse – Ellen, from Seattle, and Manou, her boyfriend from Luxembourg. When Manou suggested a round the world trip to her, she had not even ridden a motorcycle. Now, as they took on the Americas and Africa she told me she could ride the dirt and change brake pads with the best of them.

As Zoe gamely lay down on the rain-sodden dockside of the *S.S. Klondike*, instructed by me to take some interesting 'upshots' of me on the bike, a pair of GS riders sailed past. The lead rider spotted us and doubled back. Paul and Gerry, two likeable characters from Michigan were riding up to Fairbanks, Alaska. Both in their 60s, they were relishing the adventure and the break from their families. We arranged to meet that night in the TNT, a roughneck roadhouse which the pair assured me was full of interesting characters.

The 'interesting characters' of the TNT were a bunch of inebriated Hannaton Indians, staggering on and off the stage to croak drunkenly into the microphone of the karaoke machine. It seemed as though Paul and Gerry had acquired some new long-distance biking buddies. There was Giovanni, an Italian on an Africa Twin, whom they'd run into at various intervals on the Alcan, and a truly bizarre Japanese boy called Takinora, who looked like a frail, teenage girl. "I go round world – very nice." He broke into a buck-toothed grin and mimed a hunched-over-the-handlebars stance. He had left Japan 15 months previously with only the clothes he was wearing, a few words of broken English, an under-powered, home-market-only 250cc trail bike and not a lot else. He was either totally insane or the owner of melon-sized testicles. I could not work out which.

The following morning I had press interviews with both the Whitehorse Star and the Yukon Gazette, before checking out of the Yukon Inn and hitting the 350-mile trail to Dawson City. I was hoping to meet up with Paul and Gerry again, so had agreed to make a 100-mile detour to Dawson Creek, which was in line with their destination of Fairbanks.

After riding for about 349 miles in rain and only one dry mile at the very end, I decided that British bikers didn't have such a bad deal after all. Though a soft, hazy afternoon sun redeemed the day as I rode into Dawson City.

This archetypal gold rush town has the atmosphere of the Klondike in spades. Old, slightly shabby wooden buildings with raised wooden sidewalks border dirt roads. There's a nod towards tourism in the shape of themed 'Klondike Jane' type music hall, but it serves to enhance, rather than detract from the town's authenticity. The call of the wild feels strong here. Apart from the relative proximity of Jack London's cabin, in itself a testament to the remoteness of the place, the stark night-time daylight, rugged mountains and frontier town feel of Dawson make this 'the real deal'. I loved it.

I was picking up signs for Innuvik while approaching Dawson City. Innuvik has a world-renowned annual dog and sleigh race, nicely complemented by tea-boiling and muskrat-skinning competitions. So said the signs.

As I stood at the counter of an old-fashioned Dawson City saloon bar in my trail-soiled gear, sinking a Jack Daniels hopefully to drive out the bone-numbing cold, the thought occurred to me that wouldn't it be great to just slam a fistful of gold dust down on the bar in payment for your whisky. No poncing around counting your change, just: Bang! Down with the gold dust and "line up another, pardner!" Just like the old days. Then go out and skin another muskrat. I realised with resignation that neither way for me – I could not bear the thought of skinning a muskrat and would no doubt be mind-numbingly bored after a day's gold panning. My GS fulfilled me more than any horse could and all those petticoated saloon girls were probably riddled with syphilis anyway.

I took a long hot soak in the Victorian bath, trying to generate some life into my frozen skeleton. In no time I would be in Alaska, the last on the roll-call of countries and states that adorned the back of my official tour T-shirts.

*   *   *   *

Arctic dogs and small clusters of 'First Nation People' studied me as I loaded the bike. The procedure I had perfected over nearly four months was soon to become redundant. The thought saddened me. The pale grey morning sky did little to uplift me.

I took a small six-car ferry across the Yukon River. I was to join the Top of the World Highway from the other side of the river. This would take me the 200 miles to the town of Tok, Alaska.

The Top of the World Highway is cold. Damned cold. With an elevation of about 4,000 feet and a totally exposed aspect, on the wrong kind of day it could freeze your eyelids closed. And I was about to run out of petrol on it ... .

I flagged down an RV coming in the other direction. Did he know where I could get fuel? "I'm afraid it's a few miles over the US border, son," the baseball-capped retiree informed me regretfully. Vehicles passed very occasionally and when they did I flagged them down. They were either running on diesel or didn't have anything with which to effect a siphoning pipe. I figured out that if I could only reach the highest point on the road under the bike's power, I may be able to cut the engine and coast down parts of the road as it dropped down to the Alaskan US border control and – hopefully – to a gas pump.

The road did indeed drop down, in a long, steep piste, not dissimilar to the Cresta Run. The road surface was loose, fine gravel that produced huge clouds of billowing dust. To descend this incline at speed with all the engine braking and inherent control that a boxer twin configuration offers would be a white-knuckle experience. To freewheel it with no engine braking was not far short of suicidal, but I knew I would have to build up a good head of steam to give me some momentum up the other side. Guiding the bar ends lightly in my open palms I went for it, desperately avoiding touching the brakes on this loose surface. Despite a lot of snaking the bike kept a fairly true line – a great consolation with a steep drop on either side of this spinal pass.

Chapter 26

Alaska ... the Final Frontier

The tiny cluster of huts that served as US Immigration to Alaska either couldn't or wouldn't offer me fuel. Immigration controls were brief and perfunctory. Nobody in their right mind would choose a job-starved Arctic wilderness to emigrate to illegally. Why, they even pay residents a healthy 'hardship allowance' to live in this forgotten corner. Naturally, this is paid out of oil licence revenues. A family of two adults and five children can be looking at almost $14,000 per annum. In addition, anybody with more than one-eighth Indian blood (I'm not sure how they measure it) gets free medical care automatically. The goodies don't end there. Grants are available to First Nation People for fridges, TVs and microwaves. A large number of them blow their PFO grants (funded from oil drilling revenue and given to all native peoples in Alaska) on a new snowmobile which will take pride of place in

Eskimos, Alaska

the front yard of their one-storey shack alongside a selection of other disembowelled and rusting snowmobiles – legacies from previous years of PFO grants. The small change left usually ends up on the counter of the liquor store.

I deviated from the Top of the World Highway to follow a stream and minor road that looked interesting. At the junction was a grocery store-cum-everything, with a lone Flemish Belgian outside waiting expectantly for something. He told me that after an industrial accident had pensioned him off at the tender age of 40 he had decided to travel the world. He had been travelling for five years to date on a budget of £350 per month. Given that air fares etc. had to be taken out of this amount I imagined the twelve months he spent in India would have been less than comfortable. He planned to travel for another five years before settling in Australia. Belgium did not figure in his future plans as indeed didn't Colombia (my favourite country) which he was too nervous to visit. "I think zey are crazy people down there," he confided.

Two more hours of towering peaks and beautiful lakes and I arrived at the town of Tok. Nothing much to see other than a crossroads, a scattering of buildings and a gaggle of Athabascan First Nation People hanging around waiting for something to happen. In a large barn-type building I enjoyed a superbly baked Alaskan sockeye salmon, baked potato and home-made baked beans.

Fording a shallow river near Tok

Wait! Wasn't that an early BMW R80 GS I could see on the horizon, followed by an R100 GS bike and sidecar outfit? A black, leather-clad, fresh-faced girl pulled up, who from the neck down looked like Modesty Blaise, but from the neck up looked as though she had just stepped out of a milking parlour. She introduced herself as Mary from Frankfurt. The sidecar outfit followed her onto the lay-by. It was piloted by Dad, a woolly mammoth of a man in leather bib and braces, and Mum in the sidecar, who looked like the senior dairy maid. They were touring Canada and Alaska with a pair of tents. It was a foregone conclusion that I would be staying at the Tok Inn, being the only hotel in town so I invited them over for a beer that evening.

I watched Mary's power-restricted R80 GS crob, crob its way up the main drag and onto the gravel forecourt of the Tok Inn, closely followed by the great bulk of the parental sidecar outfit.

Mary spoke basic English; Mum and Dad practically nothing. Dad's five-word repertoire extended to "Isle of Man – very goot!". They'd all enjoyed a couple of jaunts to the Isle of Man TT, it transpired. There was a charming innocence and naivety about them which was very engaging. Dad attempted to explain to me that they were originally from the East German city of Dresden, before moving in 1984 to a small village near Frankfurt. Their slightly humble, ingenuous manner was maybe a legacy of half a lifetime of 'making do'.

We were joined by another woolly mammoth local in an old plaid shirt, his untamed beard brushing the fifth button down. In his inebriated state, I had difficulty understanding him, so the Germans had no hope. He did, however, eventually manage to put together a quite cohesive argument in favour of hunting as a means of constructive breed management, and the need for Alaskans to take responsibility for their own wildlife, rather than take orders from California pressure groups. After scrounging half-a-dozen cigarettes he looked to be 'on the take', but he redeemed himself by presenting me with a new bandanna – "In recognition of what you're doing, man." I was touched.

After an average breakfast served in the ludicrously overpriced Tok Inn, I contemplated my last day before reaching Anchorage. I had 340 miles ahead of me with a foreboding sky that threatened testicle-freezing misery. I was wearing thermal underwear and two pairs of silk long-johns that were practically causing me to pass out

A wandering minstrel in Palmer

in the artificial warmth of the Tok Inn. I knew it would be a different story an hour later.

The charmless Teenage Mutant Turtle who dumped my breakfast in front of me spoke only one word during the length of the service: "Yes?" I'm not even sure he said that – I think he was clearing his throat. I responded by expressing pathetic gratitude for his attentions.

I set off for Anchorage with a heavy heart – desperately sad that my journey was about to reach its conclusion. My legs were freezing and I still had another 300 miles to go – "Oh, death, where is thy sting?" People told me that South and Central Alaska were warm in August. What happened? It reassured me to discover that there were people less fortunate than I. The couple of thousand poor, miserable souls taking part in a charity bike ride between Fairbanks and Anchorage were hunched over their handlebars, grimacing at the Arctic wind in their faces. When they signed up to raise funds for an AIDS vaccine they probably imagined, like me, they were up for a brisk ride under inviting blue skies. How wrong they were. I was wearing the aforementioned two pairs of long johns, lined leather jeans and waterproof overtrousers and still my legs were freezing – wonder how they felt in Lycra shorts?

Past a huge glacier, the sight of which made me feel even colder. Through the town of Palmer, with only fifty miles to go, I hit heavy traffic outside Anchorage. Big semi trucks flung muddy, glutinous spray at me. I felt chilled to the bone, my crotch was wet due to leaking waterproofs. Frankly, I did not feel in great spirits.

And there it was ... "Welcome to Anchorage". The all-important sign that heralded the culmination of four months of excitement, trials and tribulations. From the depths of despair to the heights of euphoria. A year of planning, sleepless nights, doubt, restless anticipation, farewells ... the road ...

*   *   *   *

I was a little vague as to how my arrival should be. I watched the odometer click on to 19,052 miles – the distance I had covered since pulling out of the docks at Punta Arenas, Chile. A civic reception would be nice, or even just a TV news crew. But why should there be? As one of the great outposts of the world, Anchorage had probably seen its fair share of adventurers. And they didn't know I was coming anyway!

Before finding a hotel I had to find a copy shop. I had decided to have some postcards made up for friends and sponsors to mark the end of the journey. In Kinko's Copies I got into conversation with a cute, tomboyish girl called Kristen. She told me she was a freelance photographer and thrilled to the idea of my trip. She offered to meet me the following morning to take some shots of me on the bike for the proposed postcards. She very kindly offered to do it for free, a deal I was not about to turn down.

I had to find a place to wash the bike in readiness for the photo shoot. After riding around in the rain for another two hours I found out that people don't like to wash their vehicles in Anchorage. A further two-hour hunt for a sensibly-priced hotel was equally frustrating. I was told the prices were higher because it was 'peak season'. It was freezing cold, grey and raining solidly. What was low season like? Another few laps around this grey, utilitarian city and I eventually found an Econolodge, which as the name implies, are usually cheap. This was one of the grimmest Econolodges I had seen, and they wanted to charge me $95 a night! Half that would have been too much. I took the last dingy room and hunkered down for five days.

Places look so much better when the sun's shining – as indeed did Anchorage the following morning. I rode over to the city limits to meet Kristen by the huge 'Anchorage' sign, which seemed an appropriate place for a photo. After a successful shoot I took her out for breakfast. Kristen, like so many residents of Anchorage, is from 'somewhere else' – usually the lower forty-eight. People move to Alaska for various reasons: either to go into hiding from the law or maintenance-demanding ex-spouses, or to return to nature or live the lifestyle they please. As a lesbian, Kristen favoured the last option. At first, when she mentioned her partner, I took it to mean the business variety, but she gradually revealed her orientation, without making a big deal about it. Kristen was charming company

– bright, effervescent and enthusiastic. We made plans to go out for dinner, along with her friend, Patty.

I gave a long interview to the Alaska Daily News, where journalist, Susan Morgan, told me something about Alaskan social issues. It seems the First Nation People I had seen drinking what looked like anti-freeze out of clear plastic Pepsi bottles, aren't merely conforming to white middle-class society's view of them. They have had a rough history of both state and oil companies taking liberties with their land. Imagine how the residents of Surrey would feel if the government just ran a pipeline through their country without asking first?

After spending a half-day in the dreariest mall imaginable, full of shops selling tat, like gilt-framed, airbrush paintings of huskies and other symbolic Alaskan 'art', I decided to ride out to the Alaska State Fair to get the full flavour of the State. I was not disappointed. Where else on earth can you enjoy such spectacles as cow-milking contests, tree-felling competitions and the nail-biting tension of ... pig racing? A large percentage of visitors to the State Fair are First Nation People from the far corners of the state. If you're expecting the typical stereotype of an Eskimo hunched fishing through a hole in the ice, next to his igloo, forget it. These people drive trucks and eat at Burger King like everyone else. If anything was going to lift my melancholy mood it was the sight of four pigs wearing different coloured neckerchiefs, racing around an oval grass track, the commentator excitedly babbling into her microphone: "Yes! It's Calvin Swine now, closing up on Al Boar!" This was entertainment at its best ...

Neglecting to fasten one of my Touratech pannier lids on properly, I promptly lost it on the way back to Anchorage. Very irritating, though not as much as if I had

Calvin Swine snatching the lead from Al Boar

lost it in Punta Arenas. The fateful day came when I had to make the final ride to the 'Motorcycle Shop' in Anchorage. They replaced the whistling fuel pump, cleaned the bike, dismantled it and put it into a GS crate ready for the long journey home. I felt like hugging it in gratitude for the sterling service it had given me. Never have I felt so attached to a bike. I had spoken to Doug, the incredibly calm and efficient freight forwarder from Vancouver a couple of days previously. The bike would be road freighted to Vancouver from where it would be rail freighted across Canada to the east coast. From there it would be sea freighted to Thamesport, England and finally road freighted up to Allan Jefferies in Yorkshire, de-crated and rebuilt. It would be a good couple of months before I saw it again.

I had a couple of days left in Anchorage before flying home, so I hired a car. I felt like I'd had an arm removed without the freedom of the bike. I drove around, watched a couple of movies, spent an evening in a bar with a 250lb woman who made pornographic videos, and awaited the long journey home and back to reality. I checked out of the Vietnamese-owned and -run Econolodge and got a lift to the airport with their driver. He was a seething mass of racial hatred and spent the whole journey telling me what deceitful and dishonest people the Vietnamese were. He then made the surprising revelation that his ex-wife was Vietnamese and his son of mixed race. I suggested to him that if he had chosen to live and work with them they can't be that bad. He grunted non-committally.

A return journey from Anchorage – Seattle – Dallas – Fort Worth – Chicago – Manchester gave me plenty of time to reflect on my trip. Apart from the 19,052 miles I had clocked up, I was on my fourth set of tyres and third service. I had stopped counting the number of fill-ups I'd had a long time ago and the number of times I had dropped the bike, which still looked in remarkably good shape. I don't believe there's a new bike on earth that is better equipped for this sort of trek.

As my mother drove me up the A34 from Manchester Airport to Wilmslow, my mind wandered to the Bolivian Altiplano, Ruta 3 in Argentinian Patagonia, the Atacama Desert ... something had hanged within me: my body was on the A34 in Cheshire but my soul was out there on a lonesome road in a distant land.

Epilogue

Despite my best efforts to re-assimilate into everyday Wilmslow life, I experienced huge difficulties. The initial flurry of speaking engagements, writing this book and winding up the David Lewis Appeal kept me busy for the first few months, but the torpor that followed made me restless to change my life. To this end, I practised my Spanish and dreamt of another place ... a fresh start. Not one to do things by half, I woke up one day, decided I was going to sell my business and home, take a teaching qualification and live in Colombia – all within the year.

Just one year later, I realised my ambition and came to live in Cartagena de Indias, Colombia – drawn back to the city that intrigued me so much on my Chile-Alaska journey. I got a teaching post in a private bilingual college, as well as acting as press and public relations officer for the school and generally living the life of a Colombian. I love Colombia and Latin America in general and, despite the dramatic drop in income, have no regrets.

I had been living in Cartagena for six months when, one Sunday morning, I wandered into my favourite Internet café where – as always – sat my colleague, friend and fellow travel-writer, Australian Glen Short. Glen is something of an expert on travel literature, having read everything pertaining to Latin America that has ever been written. On this particular morning he seemed unusually animated: "Hey! Guess who's coming to Cartagena in two weeks!" he said, turning towards me from the screen, a look of boyish enthusiasm on his face. "Surprise me," I replied, mildly interested that anybody would risk a trip to Colombia on the weekend of the national elections: a notoriously volatile time. "Ted Simon, that's who," he whispered with appropriate reverence in his voice. Glen's early overlanding expeditions had germinated while reading 'Jupiter's Travels' and, like me, the book had shaped his future life to some extent.

Now, Ted Simon was doing an action re-play of his original world trip – at 70 years of age. Over the next week we followed

Ted's adventures via his website and sent him a string of e-mails offering him free accommodation ... meals ... anything to secure a visit. He responded, saying he'd love to avail himself of our hospitality. But that was before the accident. In Medellin Ted had come to grief while attempting an overtaking manoeuvre on someone who didn't want to be overtaken. Fractured bones, a badly damaged bike and a prolonged unscripted stay in Medellin, meant that Cartagena had to be shelved in favour of flying directly to Central America. He had deadlines to meet, namely the Turkey-Iran crossing before the onset of winter made the mountain pass impassable. But all was not lost. He finally agreed to fly up and see us for a long weekend.

Two weeks later, I stepped off the plane from Monteria where I had been spending a few days, and raced around to Glen's apartment, to be greeted by a greyer, beardless, but unbelievably youthful Ted Simon: 70 years old but not looking a day over 55. There were so many questions I wanted to ask him, notes to compare. I soon realised that Ted is an expert at deflecting the sort of questions he's been asked a thousand times before.

We had a good time, giving him an insider's tour of Cartagena. He came along to the Colegio Britanico where Glen and I worked, posed gamely for photographs, told the children about his adventures and, all too soon, flew on to Panama City for the next leg of his second solo round-the-world motorcycle trip.

I thought that Ted's visit might inspire me to take to the road again. I've often fancied riding down the east side of South America. But not yet ... maybe when I'm 70.